100 inventions that made history

Brilliant breakthroughs that shaped our world

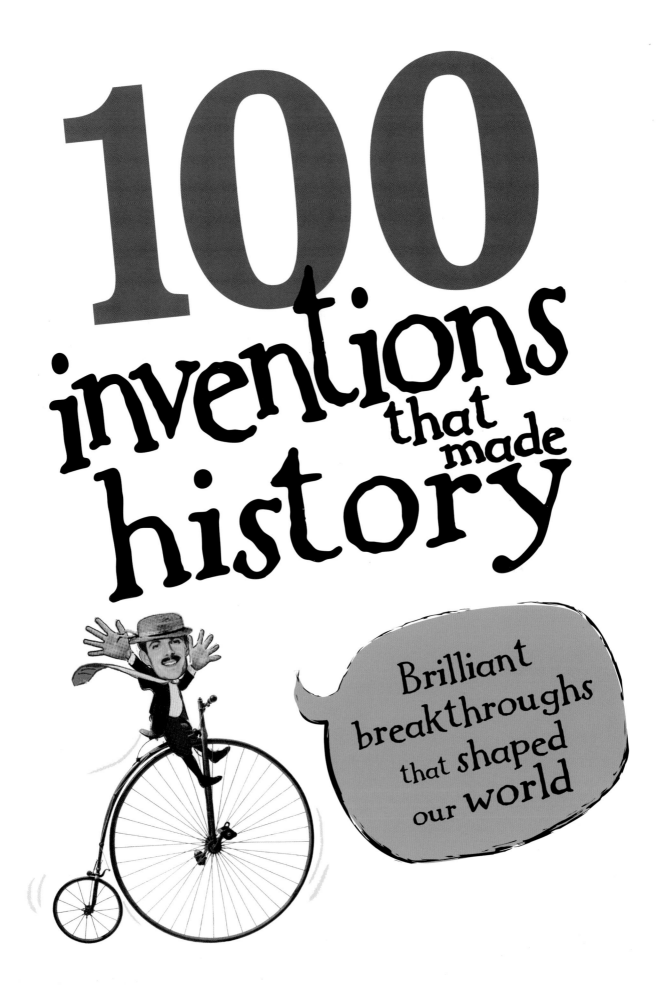

**London, New York,
Melbourne, Munich, and Delhi**

Senior Editor Jenny Sich
Senior Art Editor Stefan Podhorodecki
Project Editor Steven Carton
Designers Mary Sandberg, Jeongeun Park

Managing Editor Linda Esposito
Managing Art Editor Diane Peyton Jones
Category Publisher Andrew Macintyre

Senior Producer Gemma Sharpe
Senior Producer, Pre-production Ben Marcus
Producer, Pre-production Rachel Ng
Picture Researcher Sumedha Chopra

Jacket Editor Manisha Majithia
Jacket Designer Stefan Podhorodecki
Jacket Design Development Manager Sophia MTT

Publishing Director Jonathan Metcalf
Associate Publishing Director Liz Wheeler
Art Director Philip Ormerod

First published in Great Britain in 2014
by Dorling Kindersley Limited,
80 Strand, London WC2R 0RL

A CIP catalogue record for this book is available from the British Library.

ISBN: 978-1-40934-098-0

Hi-res workflow proofed by Altaimage, UK
Printed and bound by Hung Hing, Hong Kong

Discover more at
www.dk.com

100
inventions
that
made
history

Brilliant
breakthroughs
that shaped
our world

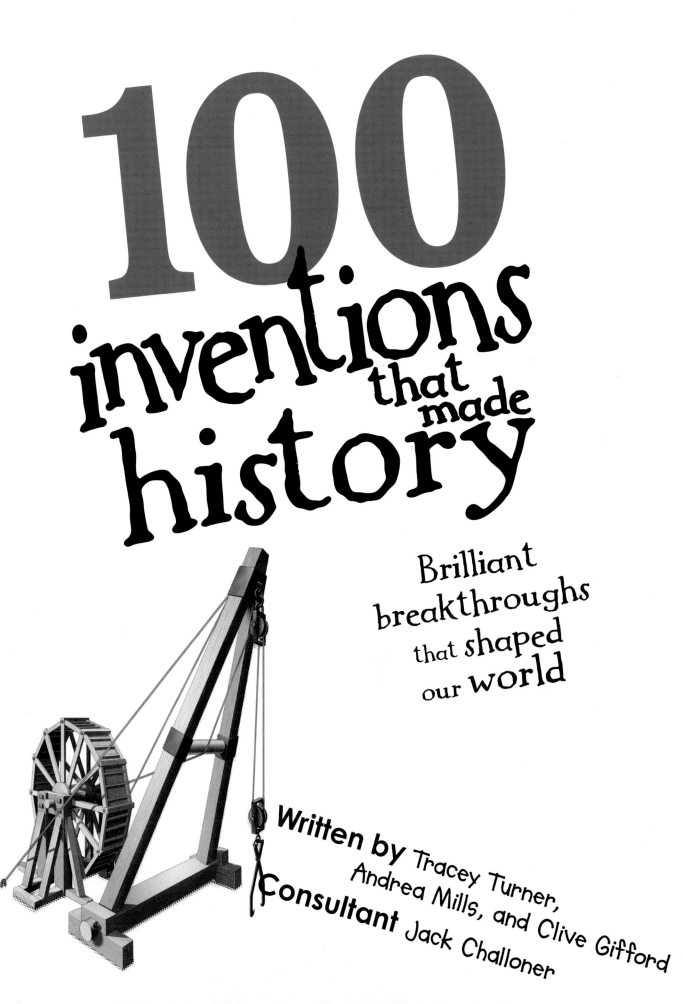

Written by Tracey Turner,
Andrea Mills, and Clive Gifford
Consultant Jack Challoner

Contents

move

A lack of transport limited movement in the past. The wheel got early civilizations rolling and hasn't stopped since, as millions take the driving seat around the world's highways and byways. From sailing the seas to swooping the skies, new modes of transport have taken us further, and sped us there faster. Our planet is now an entirely accessible world.

Rolling along

Before wheels, if you wanted to move something **enormous and heavy**, you would need some logs and *a lot of people*. You'd place the logs on the ground, slide your object on top of them, and then get your friends to use the logs to roll it along. Or you could drag a sledge. Either way, it was slow and **EXHAUSTING**!

People or animals pulled the object across the log rollers on ropes, and others pushed from behind.

The last log had to be brought around to the front as the object moved forward.

The wheel

Imagine life without wheels: no cars or bikes for a start, and no cogs and gears inside machines, either. With so many around, it might just be the most important invention of them all.

Making the world go ROUND AND ROUND

Wheely useful

Watching log rollers in action, someone, somewhere, had a *flash of inspiration*: wheels attached to axles would be **SO MUCH BETTER!** The first wheels we know about were made **5,000 years ago** in Mesopotamia (modern-day Iraq) and Slovenia. They were attached to simple carts pulled by animals, while everyone had a nice rest.

Stone wheels were used for grinding, but are too heavy to move vehicles.

It paved the way for...

GEARS AND COGS *are used in machines to* MULTIPLY FORCE, *and were first used in ancient Greece.*

Water wheels were invented in ANCIENT GREECE, *and were used to irrigate crops and grind corn.*

Bright spokes

At first, wheels were **solid discs of wood**. They worked, but they were very heavy. Around 2,000 BCE, someone in ***western Siberia*** came up with the bright idea of using spokes inside the wheels to replace the solid wood. They were **LIGHTER AND FASTER**. Metal hubs used with greased axles made wheels turn even more smoothly.

By the way...
It was Neolithic (late Stone Age) people like me who first invented the wheel. We also invented farming and developed polished tools made of stone.

It takes far less energy to turn the axle than to turn the wheel.

How it changed the world

Wheels allowed people to travel and trade much more easily than ever before, and a few thousand years later, wheels were moving faster and further than ever thanks to the engine. Wheels are also the driving force behind countless useful machines.

Did you know?
The oldest wheels ever discovered are on a stone toy. It dates from 5,500 BCE and was found in Turkey.

The Americas

The wheel **wasn't big** in the Americas – the only ones found there are on children's toys. This is probably because there were no animals strong enough to pull carts, like oxen or horses. The people there ***had to wait*** until these animals, and the wheel, were introduced to them in the 16th century. Until then, the most useful animal they had was the **LLAMA**.

SPINNING WHEELS, *used to turn plant material or wool into thread, are probably an* **INDIAN INVENTION**, *from about the 11th century.*

WHEELS *really began to motor from the 1700s, at first under steam power and later using* **PETROL ENGINES**.

Caravel

The speedy SAILING SHIP that harnessed wind power to rule the waves

Exploring the world

Ships with sails had been around for thousands of years, but caravels were the first to truly **master the seas**. Developed in the 1400s, they were light and fast, with lateen sails (triangular sails fixed to a sloping yardarm) that made them *easier to manoeuvre* than previous sailing ships. Caravels could sail **LONG DISTANCES**, opening up new possibilities for intrepid explorers.

Lateen sails allowed the ship to "tack" – sail in zigzags into the wind.

Not much room for cargo – caravels were designed for exploration.

How it changed...
European explorers used caravels to sail further than ever before, discovering new lands and opening up new trade routes.
the world

Henry the Navigator

The caravel was invented by Prince Henry of Portugal, known as Henry the Navigator, who founded a famous **NAVIGATION SCHOOL**. But, despite his name, Henry never went on a voyage of discovery in one of his ships – in fact he *never went to sea at all*.

Setting sail

Caravels were invented just in time for **Christopher Columbus** – he sailed them across the Atlantic to the Caribbean in 1492. Not long after, **EUROPEAN EXPLORERS** colonized the Americas, India, and Africa, and opened up new *trade routes*, changing the lives of many of the people who lived there.

Early subs

The world's **FIRST SUBMARINE** dived beneath the surface of the River Thames in London in 1624. It was powered by 12 oars, and its crew **breathed oxygen** produced by heating potassium nitrate. The first sub to be used in warfare was the *Turtle* (left). It was used in 1776 during the American War of Independence.

← The *Turtle* was driven by hand-operated propellers.

Submarine

DEEP-DIVING VESSELS that opened up an undersea world

How it changed...
Submarines changed the way wars were fought at sea by allowing crews to hide beneath the waves and launch surprise attacks on ships.
the world

USS *Holland* carried three torpedoes for underwater warfare.

USS *Holland* could dive 30 m (100 ft)

Holland's submarine

Submarines wouldn't have got very far or very deep using manpower alone. In 1881 Irish-American engineer **J P Holland** demonstrated a submarine called the *Fenian Ram*, which used an engine on the surface and a battery when it dived. Holland had invented the modern submarine, and supplied the **US NAVY** with its first ever sub, USS *Holland*, in 1900.

Battle stations

Submarines launched **TORPEDOES** that sank hundreds of ships in the First World War, and they've been used in *warfare* ever since. Today, most naval submarines use nuclear power and can stay **underwater for months** at a time, lurking in the depths of the ocean.

Navigational novelties

Without navigational aids, sailors would rarely sail out of sight of land.

Knowing WHERE YOU'RE GOING

Sailors would be completely lost without these ingenious inventions. They have allowed explorers to travel the world and discover new lands.

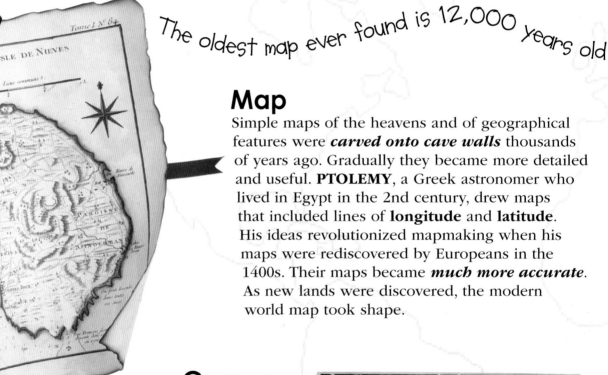

The oldest map ever found is 12,000 years old

Map

Simple maps of the heavens and of geographical features were *carved onto cave walls* thousands of years ago. Gradually they became more detailed and useful. **PTOLEMY**, a Greek astronomer who lived in Egypt in the 2nd century, drew maps that included lines of **longitude** and **latitude**. His ideas revolutionized mapmaking when his maps were rediscovered by Europeans in the 1400s. Their maps became *much more accurate*. As new lands were discovered, the modern world map took shape.

Compass

The Chinese were using compasses during the **QIN DYNASTY** (221–206 BCE) to ensure buildings were facing the right way for good fortune. The spoon-shaped needle was made from **lodestone**, a naturally magnetized mineral that always points to magnetic north. Around the *11th century*, compasses began to be used for navigation.

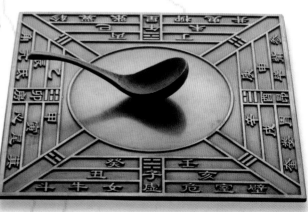

Mariner's astrolabe

Sailors used astrolabes, first made around 1300, to measure the **height of the Sun** or a particular star. This allowed them to calculate their *latitude* (north–south position). Mariner's astrolabes helped sailors **EXPLORE FAR-AWAY LANDS** in a period known as the Age of Discovery, from the 1400s to the 1600s.

Marine sextant

Sextants (meaning sixths) use **MIRRORS** to measure the angle of the Sun or the North Star in relation to the horizon at particular times of day. Like the astrolabe, this allows sailors to work out their *north–south position*. The first one was made by English astronomer **John Bird** in 1757. They are still used today – if onboard computers crash, mariners can **FIND THEIR WAY** with a sextant.

The arc of a sextant is one sixth of a circle (60 degrees)

Did you know?
Marshall Islanders memorized stick charts, made from coconut fronds, to map ocean swells and navigate the Pacific by canoe.

Satellite navigation

Today, there are *networks of satellites* in space that allow users to pinpoint their position almost anywhere on earth. A receiver compares **TIME SIGNALS** from four or more satellites. To work out its exact location, the receiver calculates the **distance to each satellite**. Today, most sailors rely on satellites to safely navigate through the world's waters – and many cars and mobile phones have satellite receivers, too.

Explosive steam engines

The power of steam was first used to pump water out of mines, but the clunky engines tended to **EXPLODE**. Englishman **Thomas Newcomen** invented a more successful version in 1712, but it was still very inefficient. In the 1770s, Scottish inventor *James Watt* improved the invention and made it much more efficient.

4. Beam connnects to a second rod, which drives the gear wheel.

3. Piston rod moves up and down, pushing on one end of a beam.

5. Heavy flywheel prevents the engine from getting stuck at the top or the bottom of each up–and–down cycle.

2. Cylinder contains a piston, which is pushed up and down by the steam, and pushes on the piston rod.

6. Gear wheel turns up–and–down motion into rotational motion, which can drive machinery.

1. Tube allows steam from heated water into the engine's cylinder.

Steam engine

The DRIVING FORCE behind the machines that powered the Industrial Revolution

Moving machines

Watt **steamed ahead**, continually improving his engine. It was used to pump water into canals and out of mines, drive bellows in iron works, and power **MACHINES** in textile mills. This rapid growth of Britain's industry was called the *Industrial Revolution*.

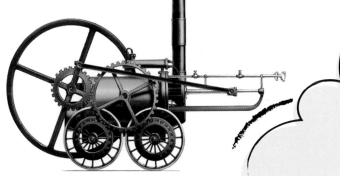

Stephenson's *Rocket*

After Trevithick's locomotive, inventors set to work designing **BETTER ONES**. *Rocket*, designed by Robert Stephenson, won a competition to find the best of the lot in 1829. It **steamed into the history** books at 48 km/h (30 mph).

Locomotion

In 1801, British engineer **Richard Trevithick** invented a steam engine that changed everything. Using *high-pressure steam*, he built a steam-powered carriage, and then in 1808 the world's first steam **RAILWAY LOCOMOTIVE**, *Catch Me Who Can*. It hauled 70 people and a load of coal along a railway track.

Connecting rods driven by pistons turned the wheels and moved the engine forwards.

Rocket hauled 13 tonnes of loaded wagons to win the 1829 competition.

ROCKET

How it changed...
Far faster and stronger than horses, steam locomotives triggered a transport revolution that sped people and goods all over the world. **the world**

Steam locomotive

The engine that put transport on the RIGHT TRACK

Building railways

The new locomotives could now transport **COAL** for the new steam-powered machines, as well as the goods they made, and thousands of kilometres of *railway tracks* began to be laid. The world's first **intercity railway**, between the UK cities of Liverpool and Manchester, was built in 1830.

The east and west coasts of the US were connected by the first transcontinental railway in 1869.

15

Electric motor

Electric motors use magnetism to produce movement. Today they are the driving force behind many everyday objects.

Getting the modern world MOVING

Nikola Tesla was an American engineer who worked on a large number of different inventions during his lifetime.

Faraday's electrical experiments

Bright spark Michael Faraday made the *first electric motor* in 1821 when he produced **CONTINUOUS MOTION** from electricity. It worked because passing **an electric current** through a wire produces magnetism. Later motors used electromagnets – coils of wire around an iron core – to make this effect stronger.

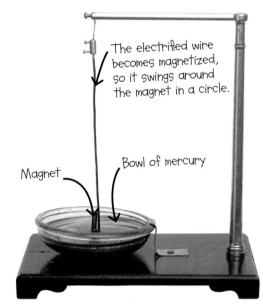

The electrified wire becomes magnetized, so it swings around the magnet in a circle.

Magnet

Bowl of mercury

By the way...
I once started a small but alarming earthquake in the course of one of my experiments, and another time made terrifying artificial lightning!

Motoring on

German engineer **MORITZ VON JACOBI** used electromagnets to make a motor powerful enough to be put to *practical use*. In a world first, an improved version of his motor drove a **paddle boat** across the River Neva in Russia in 1838 with 14 people on board.

The wire is coiled into eight electromagnets. Passing a current through the wire makes the central wheels turn.

Electric current provided by a battery travels through the wire.

It couldn't have happened without...

In 1820 **HANS OERSTED** discovered **ELECTROMAGNETISM** – that an electric current creates a magnetic field.

Also in 1820, **ANDRÉ-MARIE AMPÈRE** *worked out the relationship between the electromagnetic force and the electric current.*

16

An outer set of electromagnets (called the stator) remains stationary.

Inside the stator, a moving set of electromagnets forms the rotor.

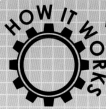

HOW IT WORKS

Motors that run on direct current have a permanent magnet and an electromagnetic rotor. The rotor's north and south poles are attracted to the opposite poles of the permanent magnet, so the rotor moves half a turn. The direction of the current is then reversed so the rotor moves another half turn. Continually switching the current like this keeps the motor spinning. Motors that use AC work in a similar way but they do not need a mechanism to reverse the current.

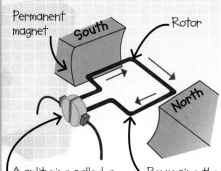

Permanent magnet

South

Rotor

North

A split ring called a commutator switches the current's direction.

Reversing the current reverses the rotor's magnetic poles, making it move half a turn.

The rotor can be attached to machinery, such as a fan or a conveyor belt.

Tesla's induction motor

Nikola Tesla invented the electric motors that power large machines today. His induction motor, invented in 1887, runs on mains power, which is "alternating current" (AC) – electric current that changes direction many times a second – rather than the direct current (DC) provided by a battery.

How it changed

Electric motors took over from clunky steam engines to power machines. Now they also power the appliances we plug in and switch on every day.

the world

It paved the way for...

Steam-powered **WASHING MACHINES** *were laundering clothes in the 1800s but electric motors made them smaller and more convenient.*

ELECTRIC CARS *were first invented in the 19th century, but only now do they look set to rival petrol-powered ones.*

Bicycle

The two-wheeled way of getting people MOVING

Bicycles started off without pedals, then got too big, but developed into the perfect way to travel.

The rider sat high up over the large front wheel. →

Did you know?
Getting on a high-wheeler was difficult, stopping could be hazardous, and a pothole in the road often meant going headfirst over the handlebars. Ouch!

Velocipedes

The world's first bicycle was invented in 1818. Known as a **velocipede**, the wooden, **iron-wheeled** machine had a brake but no pedals – it had to be pushed along by the **RIDER'S FEET**. The machine was popular, but only for a few months.

Pedal power

The first successful **pedal-driven bicycle** was invented by Frenchman Pierre Lallement in about 1864. People pedalled around quite quickly, but very uncomfortably. The bicycles became known as **boneshakers** because their heavy iron frames and iron-rimmed wheels juddered over every bump and hole in the road – and back then there were **A LOT OF BUMPS AND HOLES!**

High-wheelers were also called penny-farthings, after two coins of different sizes.

It paved the way for...

German engineer **GOTTLIEB DAIMLER** *designed the first* **TWO-WHEELED MOTORCYCLE** *in 1885, in order to test out a new engine.*

BMX, *short for bicycle motocross, began in the 1970s as a pedal-power version of* **OFF-ROAD MOTORCYCLING.**

High-wheelers

Early bicycles were powered by the **front wheel**, so its size limited how fast they could go. Thrill-seekers solved the problem by making bikes with enormous front wheels – some were **1.5 m (5 ft)** across – and a much smaller rear wheel. Daredevil riders perched precariously over the front wheel and **WHIZZED ALONG** at high speeds, to the alarm of passers-by.

Today there are twice as many bicycles as cars

How it changed the world

Before bicycles, you needed a horse if you wanted to get anywhere in a hurry. Bikes speed people to their destinations without anyone cleaning up after them. They convert human power into movement more efficiently than anything else.

Safety bikes

Perilous penny farthings were replaced by **safety bicycles** in the 1880s. They were driven by a rear-wheel chain, so the wheels could be of *equal size*. Things got even better for cyclists with the invention of air-filled tyres, gears, safety reflectors, and generator-powered headlamps. **LESS WEIGHTY AND MORE EFFICIENT** models of bicycle continue to be developed.

THE TANDEM *is an unusual bicycle created for two riders to sit one in front of the other and cycle* **SIMULTANEOUSLY.**

BICYCLE RACING *is a popular* **MODERN SPORT**, *with many different events for different types of bicycle raced over various distances.*

Elevator

The invention that moved people UP in the world

As elevators gave people a safe lift to the top, buildings began to grow taller, and the shape of city skylines changed forever.

Ends of the spring jam into these strong metal teeth if the rope breaks.

By the way...
In a dramatic display, I went up on an open-sided elevator, then had someone chop through the rope with an axe!

Steam elevators

Until **steam power** gave everybody a much needed rest, the only way to lift something was for **PEOPLE OR ANIMALS** to hoist it on ropes or carry it up stairs. One of the first steam elevators was used to haul **blocks of ice** from the Hudson River in the USA in 1754.

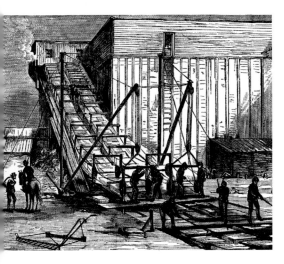

Otis demonstrated his invention in front of an amazed audience at a fair in 1854.

Did you know?
The world's tallest building at 828 m (2,716 ft), the Burj Khalifa in Dubai has a total of 57 elevators and two escalators.

Safety hoist

Elevators were not used to lift people because of the risk of the **rope snapping**. American inventor **ELISHA GRAVES OTIS** solved the problem in 1853 with his safety hoist. If the cable broke, the car still didn't fall. The first passenger lift, driven by steam power, was installed in a New York department store in 1857. It climbed **five storeys in one minute**.

Early elevators

The **ARCHIMEDES SCREW** was an ancient device used to lift water up from one level to another. It was invented in about the **3RD CENTURY BCE**.

A **HAND-POWERED LIFTING DEVICE** was invented by German engineer **KONRAD KYESER** in the early 1400s.

Electrified elevators

Steam elevators puffed away until the 1880s when the first electric elevator was installed. **Electric-powered pulleys** at the top of the shaft meant that elevators could climb **HIGHER AND FASTER** than they did in the past. Elevators were developed to become *automatic*, with passengers able to call an elevator and specify a floor at the push of a button.

Hoisting rope pulls the elevator up and pulls the springs taut at the same time. If the rope breaks, the safety mechanism kicks in.

Two sturdy springs on top of the lifting platform are kept taut by the rope, but get stuck in the metal teeth if the rope snaps.

How it changed

Elevators allowed cities to grow upwards instead of sideways. This saved precious space where land was already in short supply. High-rise living is set to get higher still as new carbon-fibre cables enable longer elevators to travel further.

the world

People and objects riding on the platform were safe at last.

357.   THE CONWAY BUILDING, CHICAGO.

Skyscrapers

Now that people could scale tall buildings quickly and safely, **skyscrapers** began to reach higher and higher, transforming cities. Chicago's **CONWAY BUILDING**, now known as the Burnham Center, is one example. When completed in 1913, it stood *91 m (300 ft)* tall.

Into the future...

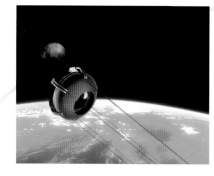

A **SPACE ELEVATOR** *could one day be available to carry people into space without a rocket. The elevator would use a super-strong, super-light* CARBON-FIBRE CABLE.

Steaming along

The first *automobile* was steam-powered, built by Frenchman Nicolas-Joseph Cugnot in 1769. However, steam engines are **HUGE**, and German engine designer Karl Benz was convinced that smaller, more efficient, **internal combustion engines** would do a better job.

Cugnot's vehicle had two wheels at the back, and one at the front.

The steam boiler was at the front.

Benz's Patent Motorwagen No. 3 had three wheels and an engine in the rear.

Driving the greatest transport REVOLUTION

Car

It's the four-wheeled wonder that takes us on countless journeys every day.

A 250

Around the Benz

Karl Benz made his first automobile in 1885, which featured steel and wood panels for the body, and steel wheels covered in rubber. To demonstrate how well the new machine worked, his wife and business partner Bertha Benz *took off on the world's first long-distance car journey*, a 200-km (124-mile) round trip. During the expedition, she used a hatpin to clear a fuel line, invented brake linings, and insulated a wire with her underwear. Everyone was amazed by her adventure, and **THE CAR BECAME A SUCCESS**.

Did you know?
The number of cars on the world's roads passed the one billion mark in 2010.

It paved the way for...

MARY ANDERSON *made it safer to drive in the rain when she invented the first* WINDSCREEN WIPERS *in 1903.*

The first ELECTRIC TRAFFIC LIGHTS *started controlling traffic in 1912 in Salt Lake City, USA, invented by policeman* LESTER WIRE.

Ford's revolution

American inventor **Henry Ford** wanted to make cars cheap and easy to run, and earn lots of money in the process. He invented the first **CONVEYOR-BELT-BASED** assembly line in 1913 at his car-manufacturing plant in Michigan, where his most famous car, the Model T, could be put together in just over 90 minutes. During the 20th century other manufacturers copied Ford, and cars **sold in their millions**.

By the way...
The Bertha Benz Memorial Route opened in 2008 in Germany – now everyone can follow in my tyre tracks.

How it changed the world

Cars allowed individuals to travel wherever they wanted, and became the world's most popular transport. As a result, cities became bigger as people could live further from work, though pollution from car exhaust fumes has meant that the environment has suffered.

HOW IT WORKS

In an internal combustion engine, fuel burns (combusts) inside tubes called cylinders, producing hot gases that push pistons. The pistons turn a crankshaft that makes the car's wheels move in a four-stroke cycle. The fuel in most engines these days is petrol.

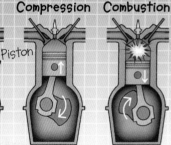

1. Intake
A mixture of air and petrol enters the chamber.

2. Compression
The piston compresses the mixture making it very hot.

3. Combustion
Spark plug ignites the mixture and drives the piston.

4. Exhaust
Gases from the explosion are expelled through the exhaust.

Piston

Chamber

Crankshaft

CAR SEAT BELTS *have been keeping drivers and passengers safe since the early 20th century.*

SAFETY STUDS *in the middle of the road that reflect car headlights, known as "CAT'S EYES", were invented in 1933 by Percy Shaw.*

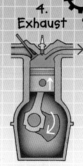

Aeroplane

The first aeroplane blazed a trail for supersonic jets and spacecraft, and helped to make the world a much smaller place.

Did you know?
The Wrights' first flight only lasted 12 seconds and covered 36.5 m (120 ft).

Taking off

People had been trying to take to the skies for hundreds of years, with some even **donning feathers and then leaping from heights**. More successfully, the first **HOT-AIR BALLOON** went up in 1783, and the first passenger-carrying glider took off in 1849. But no one had mastered *powered flight*.

By the way...
My brother Orville flew the plane after my attempt stalled. We flipped a coin to see who would get the first go.

The Wrights' flight

The American brothers **WILBUR AND ORVILLE WRIGHT** had been fascinated with flight ever since their dad gave them a toy flier. They studied gliders and *built their own*. But the Wrights' glider had an extra element: an engine to propel it. In 1903, they made the first ever **powered flight**.

It paved the way for...

British engineer Frank Whittle invented the JET ENGINE in 1930.

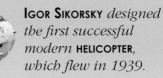

IGOR SIKORSKY *designed the first successful modern* HELICOPTER, *which flew in 1939.*

Modern-day flying

The Wrights' plane used a petrol engine that turned **propellers**. The invention of more powerful **JET ENGINES** – usually situated on the wings – made big, passenger-carrying aircraft possible. People could then jet off on flights to the other side of the world, reaching destinations that would have taken *months by sea*.

The Wright Flyer (as it came to be known) was made from spruce wood.

How it changed the world

The invention of the aeroplane made travelling across the world a lot easier. Only four decades after the first powered flight, flying machines were blasting into space.

HOW IT WORKS

Thrust from the engine drives the plane forwards, and the plane's shape lets air flow around it with minimum drag. The weight of the plane pulls it downwards, and must be overcome by lift. This is provided by the way air moves around the wings.

Lift keeps the plane in the air.

Thrust propels the plane forwards.

Drag reduces thrust.

The plane's weight must be counteracted by lift.

The **HARRIER JUMP JET** *was the first vertical take-off plane. It first flew in 1966.*

American astronaut **NEIL ARMSTRONG** *stood on the Moon after* **ROCKETING INTO SPACE** *in 1969.*

Helicopter
The amazing aircraft that put people into a SPIN

It took many attempts to get a helicopter into the air. Once it got there, however, it performed aerial acrobatics that left planes standing.

Leonardo's aerial screw used a revolving platform to make it rise upwards.

This rescue helicopter is designed to hold four crew and up to six additional people.

Aerial screw

More than **400 years** before the first helicopter flew, Italian genius Leonardo da Vinci drew plans for his "**AERIAL SCREW**", which was designed to be hand-powered by four pilots. It was never built, and modern scientists believe it would have been *too heavy* to get off the ground.

Did you know?
Leonardo's instructions stated that the aerial screw should be made of reed, wire, and linen for the screw's sail.

Autogyro

The **AUTOGYRO** was invented in 1923 by Spanish engineer Juan de la Cierva. Like a helicopter, it has a spinning rotor that keeps it airborne. Unlike a helicopter, it is *propelled by the engine*, and not the rotors – which means it can't do the tricks a helicopter can.

Early attempts...

In 1907, Frenchman **PAUL CORNU'S** helicopter rose 30 cm (1 ft) off the ground.

Another French inventor, **ETIENNE OEHMICHEN**, *created a helicopter that flew 1 km (3,280 ft) in 1924.*

By the way...
I gave up on my ideas for helicopters for 20 years when my early attempts were unsuccessful.

The amazing manoeuvrability of helicopters means they can do many things that planes can't, making them ideal for difficult rescue missions, especially on mountains and at sea. They can also do some pretty amazing stunts!

HOW IT WORKS

A helicopter's main rotor blades provide lift. The pilot can move the aircraft up, down, backwards, and forwards by changing the rotors' speed and angle (via the swash plate assembly) in relation to the wind. Hovering happens when the lift from the rotor equals the pull of gravity. The tail rotor stops the helicopter from spinning, and controls the left and right movement of the craft.

Rotor mast
Rotor blade
Swash plate assembly

Take off!

The first **practical helicopter** got off the ground in the early 1930s, but it was Russian-American Igor Sikorsky's VS-300 that today's helicopters are based on. It used a **LARGE ROTOR** on top for lift, and a tail rotor to keep it steady. It first flew in 1939, and was soon wowing onlookers. Its novel design meant that it **could move in almost any direction** (even upside down), and hover.

Sikorsky later designed the VS-44, a flying boat for passengers.

It paved the way for...

The **HOVERCRAFT**, which also uses high-pressure air to create lift, was developed by Englishman Christopher Cockerell in 1956.

Twin-rotor helicopters, such as **CHINOOKS**, were invented in the 1960s by American Frank Piasecki.

Rocket

The first rockets whizzed Chinese fireworks into the sky a thousand years ago. Now they send people into space.

It is ROCKET SCIENCE, actually!

By the way... My V-2 rocket flew at more than 5,500 km/h (3,420 mph), and delivered a ton of explosives.

Wernher von Braun led the team behind the first US satellite and the Moon landings.

We have lift off!

To **soar into the sky**, a rocket needs enough fuel to lift its weight, have a safe way of burning that fuel very quickly, and be able to work in an airless environment if it gets to space. American scientist **Robert Goddard** was the first to solve these problems: he launched the world's first liquid-fuelled rocket in 1926. It was light, but packed enough oomph to just about **get it off the ground**, though it didn't reach space.

Wernher's V-2

People realized that rockets could be used both to send humans into space and to fire as **weapons**. German Wernher von Braun's **V-2 rocket** was first used in 1944 during the Second World War. After Germany was defeated in the war, von Braun moved to the USA and pursued his dream of developing rockets for **SPACE TRAVEL**.

It paved the way for...

The **V-2** was the first ballistic missile. The first intercontinental ballistic missile, the **SOVIET R-7**, was launched in 1957.

The **MARINER 2**, launched by a rocket, became the first space probe to visit another planet when it reached **VENUS** in 1962.

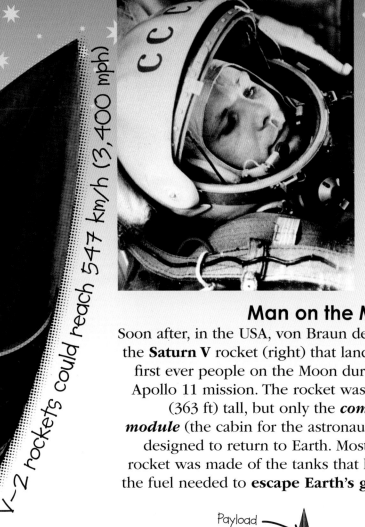

V-2 rockets could reach 547 km/h (3,400 mph)

Soviet rockets

The **USSR** (modern-day Russia and other east European countries) blasted the first satellite into space in 1957 using the Sputnik rocket, designed by **Sergey Korolev**. Korolev also developed the Vostok rocket, which zoomed the first human being, *Yuri Gagarin* (left), into orbit in 1961.

Man on the Moon

Soon after, in the USA, von Braun designed the **Saturn V** rocket (right) that landed the first ever people on the Moon during the Apollo 11 mission. The rocket was 111 m (363 ft) tall, but only the *command module* (the cabin for the astronauts) was designed to return to Earth. Most of the rocket was made of the tanks that housed the fuel needed to **escape Earth's gravity**.

HOW IT WORKS

All rockets burn fuel, either solid or liquid, to provide thrust. V-2 rockets used liquid fuel and liquid oxygen. These are stored in big fuel tanks. They are mixed together in the combustion chamber and burned to become hot gas. The gas is then pushed out of the back of the engine to drive the rocket forward.

Payload

Guidance system

Fuel tank

Liquid oxygen

Combustion chamber

Explosion provides thrust

How it changed

Rockets have transported people outside Earth's atmosphere for the first time, leading us to discover more about the Universe, and our place in it.

the world

The USSR's **Mir** space station was assembled in stages in space. It was manned for most of its **15-year** life.

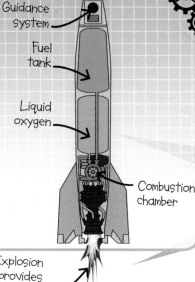

The **USA's** reusable space shuttle was launched exactly 20 years after **Yuri Gagarin** became the first person in space.

Nuclear energy

The EXPLOSIVE POWER of the atom

Nuclear technology releases the energy locked up inside atoms. The power this generates could one day zoom spaceships beyond our Solar System.

Did you know?
Another type of nuclear reaction fuses nuclei together. Nuclear fusion could provide safe, clean, and almost limitless electricity here on Earth.

Project Orion was a 1950s design for a nuclear spacecraft.

Nuclear rockets
In the future, nuclear-powered rockets could **take us to the stars**. The further away from the Sun a rocket goes, the less use solar panels become, while traditional rocket fuels **weigh a lot and run out quickly**. Nuclear energy produces much more **PROPULSION POWER** than traditional rocket fuels, so scientists are looking to nuclear power to travel **further into space than ever before**.

It paved the way for...

NUCLEAR WEAPONS *were developed in the 1940s. Two* **FISSION BOMBS** *were dropped on Japan in 1945 with devastating consequences.*

The first **NUCLEAR POWER STATION** *began generating electricity in 1954 in* **OBNINSK**, *outside Moscow in modern-day Russia.*

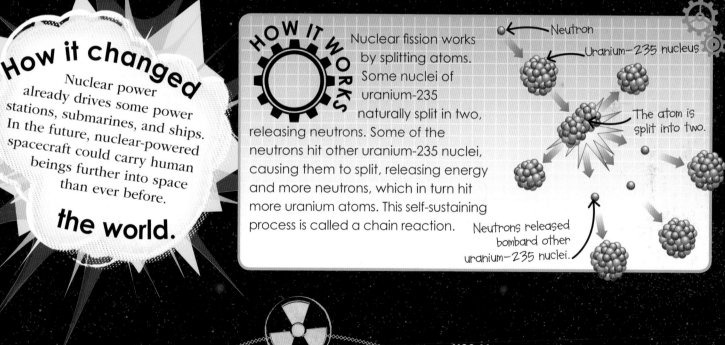

Future nuclear-powered rockets could one day take humans to Mars.

Atomic explorers

By 1900, scientists knew that everything is made from *tiny particles called atoms*. In 1909, New Zealand-born scientist **Ernest Rutherford** showed that atoms have a central nucleus, orbited by smaller particles called electrons. Later, discoveries by Rutherford and English physicist **James Chadwick** identified protons and neutrons, which make up the nucleus of an atom.

Electrons orbit the nucleus

Neutron

Proton

Lise Meitner and Otto Hahn in their laboratory, Germany, in 1913.

Nuclear fission

The **POWER OF ATOMS** was unleashed in 1938 by scientists **Lise Meitner, Otto Hahn**, and **Fritz Strassman**: they split the nucleus of a uranium atom by firing neutrons at it. As the nucleus split, some of its mass was converted into heat, a process that became known as nuclear fission. *Enrico Fermi*, an Italian scientist living in the USA, headed the team that created the first controlled **FISSION CHAIN REACTION** in the first ever **nuclear reactor**.

How it changed the world.

Nuclear power already drives some power stations, submarines, and ships. In the future, nuclear-powered spacecraft could carry human beings further into space than ever before.

HOW IT WORKS

Nuclear fission works by splitting atoms. Some nuclei of uranium-235 naturally split in two, releasing neutrons. Some of the neutrons hit other uranium-235 nuclei, causing them to split, releasing energy and more neutrons, which in turn hit more uranium atoms. This self-sustaining process is called a chain reaction.

Neutron

Uranium-235 nucleus

The atom is split into two.

Neutrons released bombard other uranium-235 nuclei.

USS NAUTILUS, *the first* **NUCLEAR-POWERED SUBMARINE**, *was launched in 1954. The icebreaker* **LENIN** *was the first* **NUCLEAR SURFACE SHIP**.

Getting

The modern world is in constant contact thanks to this bunch of groundbreaking technology. Whether reading the latest news on the Internet, chatting on the phone, or singing along to the radio, our methods of staying tuned and keeping in touch are the result of brain-boggling inventions that put us all on the same wavelength.

Paper

Helping people to make their MARK

When it first appeared around two thousand years ago, paper made writing and reading easier than ever before.

Chinese paper

Before paper was invented, people struggled with heavy books made of bamboo or spent fortunes on **expensive silk**. Legend has it that Chinese politician Ts'ai Lun revealed his paper-making technique to his **EMPEROR** in 105 CE, but even older paper, from about 100 BCE, has been discovered. *It took hundreds of years* for the secrets of paper-making to spread to other parts of Asia and North Africa, and more than 1,000 years for it to reach Europe.

The write stuff

The very **FIRST WRITTEN WORDS** were scratched onto clay slabs in ancient Mesopotamia (modern-day Iraq) more than *five thousand years ago*. Later, people wrote on silk, bone, and bamboo in China, animal skin in Europe, and papyrus in Egypt. The Aztecs and Mayans in south and central America wrote on a type of paper made from the **bark of the amate tree**.

Plant fibres are cooked with lye (a cleaning agent) before being rinsed and beaten into a pulp.

The pulp is spread over a wooden screen, like a flat, square sieve.

It paved the way for...

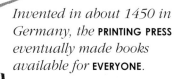

Invented in about 1450 in Germany, the **PRINTING PRESS** *eventually made books available for* **EVERYONE**.

The first **PAPER MONEY** *was used in China in the* **800s**, *but didn't reach Europe until the 1600s.*

By the way...
My special paper-making recipe included tree bark, fibres from the bamboo plant, some silk rags I had lying about, and even old fishing nets.

Ts'ai Lun was a court official during the Han dynasty.

How it changed the world

Paper made information, stories, and ideas storable on a light, strong, cheap, and space-saving surface. Without it, the printing press would never have made books and reading so popular.

Making paper

The paper-making process **HASN'T CHANGED MUCH** since Ts'ai Lun's time. Plant or textile fibres are still mashed up into a pulp, which is then sieved to create a wet sheet, and then pressed to dry it. The main difference is that **machines do it for us these days** – the first paper-making machine was invented in 1798. Also, from the 19th century, paper began to be made from wood pulp, which made it cheap enough to get *almost everyone scribbling*.

紙壓簾覆

乾焙火透

The pulp is pressed to squeeze the water out, leaving a sheet of paper.

The paper is fully dried by hanging it up on a wall.

Did you know?
Ts'ai Lun's discovery made him very famous and wealthy in China, and helped spread Chinese culture far and wide.

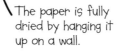

TEABAGS *first went on sale in 1903. At first, they were made from* **SILK**, *but now they're made from paper.*

PAPER TISSUES *were available from the 1920s and gradually replaced* **CLOTH HANDKERCHIEFS**.

Printing press

The start of a READING REVOLUTION

Books were once an expensive rarity, but the printing press turned them into a means of spreading ideas and information far and wide.

The lever turns a screw to raise and lower the press.

Chinese printing

People in China were turning the pages of books printed using **WOODEN BLOCKS** more than 1,000 years ago. Later, they invented *movable type* – raised letters that could be moved into place and used to print more than one book. But the **sheer number of characters** in the Chinese language complicated the process and the idea did not catch on.

This Bible in Latin from 1455 is one of Gutenberg's first printed books.

It paved the way for...

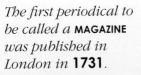

*The first printed **NEWSPAPER** was published in **1605** in Strasbourg, Germany.*

*The first periodical to be called a **MAGAZINE** was published in London in **1731**.*

Impressive press

Around 1450, German publisher **Johannes Gutenberg** invented a printing press based on olive and wine presses. His *mechanical movable type* system used metal letters arranged as required and inked by hand. **LOWERING THE PRESS** pushed the paper onto the letters and the page was printed.

The tympan (the wooden frame that holds a sheet of paper) folds over onto the inked letters.

Hand-held ink balls are used to apply ink to metal letters arranged in the forme (tray).

The tympan and forme slide under the press.

By the way...
Even though my invention changed the world, I fell out with my business partners and hardly made any money out of it.

Printing today

Within Gutenberg's lifetime his press produced books in cities **all over Europe**. He'd designed it so well that it hardly changed for the next **300 years**. From the 1800s, steam-powered presses churned out books more cheaply than ever before. Modern presses (above), powered by electricity, use rollers and **PRINT IN COLOUR**.

How it changed

Before Gutenberg's invention, books were rare and expensive because they had to be copied out by hand. The printing press meant entire books could be printed cheaply and quickly, putting ideas and information into the hands of ordinary people, not just the very rich. Millions of people learned to read as a result and discovered the pleasure of a good book.

the world

PENGUIN BOOKS

Huntingtower

WILLIAM FAULKNER

JOHN BUCHAN

PAPERBACK BOOKS *were mass produced from the* **19TH CENTURY** *on steam-powered presses.*

The first **EBOOK READERS** *were launched in* **1998**. *Ebooks will soon overtake sales of physical books.*

Telegraph

Tapping out the first ever
LONG-DISTANCE electrical messages

By the way...
My partner Mr Cooke had the initial vision for the telegraph. I used my technical skills to help him realize his ideas.

A grid of letters was used to spell out the messages received.

Communication problems
Long-distance communication took the form of smoke signals, beacons, or carrier pigeons until 1792, when a semaphore telegraph system was invented by Frenchman **CLAUDE CHAPPE**. It used pairs of moveable arms on station buildings (above) to represent letters and numbers to signal to the next station in the chain, but it was slow and **expensive to build**.

Wheatstone and Cooke's telegraph used two rows of buttons to spell out a message to send.

Electric telegraphs
English inventors William Fothergill Cooke and Charles Wheatstone came up with the first electrical long-distance communication in 1837. Their **TELEGRAPH** could send messages through an electric wire without having to be within sight of the person receiving it. Americans Samuel Morse and Alfred Vail later developed *a code of dots and dashes* that became standard telegraph code.

How it changed...
The telegraph made it possible to send almost-instant messages across oceans and continents, starting a revolution in communication. **the world**

Telegraph takeover
In 1866, Europe and North America were linked when the first **transatlantic cables** were laid. Telegraph wires reached Australia six years later, and telegraphs could be sent all around the world when cable was laid under the **PACIFIC OCEAN** in 1902.

Louis Braille

Born in France in 1809, **LOUIS BRAILLE** was blinded in an accident when he was very young. At school he wanted to read books, but there **weren't any for blind people**. When he went to a special school for blind children in Paris at the age of 10, there were books with raised letters that could be read by touch, but there were only a few, and they were **very hard to read**.

By the way... At school, I heard about a special way of communicating that could be read in the dark, which inspired me to come up with my alphabet.

Louis Braille was blinded after an accident in his father's workshop when he was three.

Louis' alphabet

Braille was **DETERMINED** to find a better way to read. When he was just fifteen he invented a system of **raised dots** arranged in rectangles, with different patterns for each letter. The Braille alphabet was simple to read and cheap to produce, and was soon **transforming lives**.

Braille

The key that unlocked the world of reading for MILLIONS of blind people

How it works

Nearly **200 years** after Braille came up with his alphabet, people are still using it, even with computers. Braille computer displays use **electro-mechanically** controlled pins to make Braille characters that can be touched. Research into how to make the Internet more accessible to blind people is underway, with Braille's alphabet **AT THE FRONT** of the new technology.

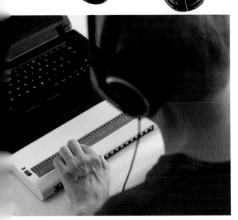

How it changed... Braille's system opened the doors of literature and education for blind people – making it easier for them to live a happy and full life. **the world**

Phonograph

The invention that brought MUSIC to our ears

Early record players, known as phonographs, were able to record and play sound back. Thomas Edison struck the first note.

Sound signals

Thomas Edison, the **famous American inventor**, made an exciting discovery while working on a recorder for telegraph signals in 1877. He realized that the indentations made by the signals **PRODUCED SOUND** when a needle ran back over them. So he set to work using cylinders wrapped in tinfoil, a metal disc, a handle, and a needle, and invented the phonograph, the *first machine to record sound*.

The horn is used to both record sound, and amplify sound when played back.

Rotating cylinder plays sounds when the handle is turned.

Flat discs soon became the most popular listening format.

Did you know?
Thomas Edison thought that teaching would be a more popular use of his invention than listening to music.

EDISON STANDARD PHONOGRAPH

Spinning discs

Edison's **foil-wrapped cylinders** were absolutely amazing, but they were a bit bulky, and could be played only a few times before decaying. In 1887, German-American inventor Emil Berliner invented a machine that traced sound grooves *onto a flat disc* instead of onto a cylinder. Lots of copies of the disc could be made – they were the **FIRST RECORDS**.

It paved the way for...

VINYL RECORDS *became very popular in the middle of the 20th century and are still* MADE TODAY.

The first COMPACT AUDIO CASSETTES *were released in 1962, originally intended for dictation machines.*

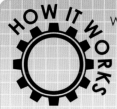
When Edison spoke into the horn, the pressure of his voice caused the needle to scratch indentations into the tinfoil-coated cylinder as it rotated. When the needle was moved over the indentations it had scratched into the foil, it played back the sound of Edison's voice through the horn, which magnified the sound.

Needle

The needle moved up and down in the dents to reproduce the sound.

Rotation of cylinder

How it changed the world

It's hard to imagine life without a soundtrack of your favourite songs, but before the phonograph, you had to make your own music or go to concerts to hear them. Recorded sound meant that at last everyone could listen to the world's greatest music in their homes.

Into the groove

As time passed, **FURTHER IMPROVEMENTS** were made to both the records and the players. The grooves on records became thinner, so more sound could fit on each disc. **Loudspeakers** replaced the horns of the early phonographs to amplify the sound. With these improvements, records were finally sounding great, and people started collecting music from their **favourite musicians**.

Incredible Edison

Though he ended up with more than a *thousand inventions* to his name, Edison considered the phonograph to be his favourite invention. He set up his own record label, **EDISON RECORDS**, to publish new recordings – first on cylinders, and later on discs. He continually improved the phonograph **right up until his death** in 1931.

By the way...
I was very hard of hearing, which helped me to concentrate – maybe that's why I never invented a hearing aid!

COMPACT DISCS *were invented in 1965 but didn't become popular until they were* **MASS-PRODUCED** *in the 1980s.*

MP3 PLAYERS *were invented in the late 1990s, making it possible to take your* **ENTIRE MUSIC COLLECTION** *with you wherever you go.*

Telephone

The invention that got people TALKING

Though who invented it is still debated, everyone agrees that the telephone revolutionized communication.

Bell's telephone

Seeking to **improve the telegraph** in 1875, Scottish inventor Alexander Graham Bell stumbled on a discovery of far greater importance. He realized that sounds could travel **ALONG THE TELEGRAPH WIRES**, and be heard in another room. Bell's first message to his assistant, Thomas Watson, was *"Mr Watson, come here! I want to see you!"*.

Bell's interest in sound and communication was inspired by his mother and wife, who were both deaf.

This version of Bell's phone was made to demonstrate the invention to Queen Victoria of the UK in 1878.

It paved the way for...

THE TELEPHONE EXCHANGE *meant that more than one phone could be connected along the same line, less than a year after the phone was invented.*

In 1889, a PUBLIC COIN-PAY TELEPHONE *was installed at the Hartford Bank in Hartford, Connecticut, USA.*

Patent fight

Bell began working up his idea and **PATENTED** it in 1876, as he knew other inventors were working on similar designs. His early phones featured a **lever to call the other phone** on the line, and a receiver that functioned as both an earpiece to hear the person on the other end and a mouthpiece to talk to them (though separate ear and mouthpieces were soon developed). It was a *roaring success*.

HOW IT WORKS

Early telephones used a thin metal disc that vibrated when someone spoke into the transmitter, making fluctuations in a layer of carbon granules. This varied the electric current, provided by a battery, which then travelled across the telephone line to the receiver. The electric current caused the carbon grains in the receiver to vibrate and copy the original sound.

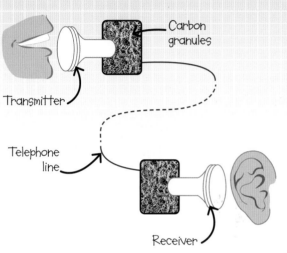

Carbon granules

Transmitter

Telephone line

Receiver

By the way...
I patented a device much like a telephone five years before Bell did. But I was too poor to pay the $10 fee to renew my patent, so I lost it.

Meucci constructed a telephone-like device at home to talk to his wife, who was ill at the time.

Mad Meucci

As Bell's telephone industry took off, a few of his rival inventors argued that he had **taken their ideas**. Among these was the Italian **ANTONIO MEUCCI**, who had demonstrated his "teletrofono" in 1860, which Bell had seen. Meucci was in the process of suing Bell, but his *legal claim ended* when he died in 1889.

How it changed the world

By turning sound into electrical signals and back again, the telephone enabled people to talk to one another over long distances for the first time. It has become the most widely used communication device on Earth.

In 1963, the first electronic **PUSH-BUTTON TELEPHONES** were offered by **BELL TELEPHONE**, the firm set up by *Alexander Graham Bell.*

Modern **SMARTPHONES** *feature touchscreens and cameras, and can connect to the* **INTERNET**.

Radio

The wireless TECHNOLOGY that everyone's tuned into

By sending signals using invisible waves instead of wires, radio reached around the world.

Marconi's 1902 magnetic detector radio used an iron-wire band wound around two pulleys to pick up signals.

Marconi's radio

Guglielmo Marconi, a 19-year-old Italian, was *fascinated* when he read about the discovery of radio waves by German scientist Henrich Hertz. Hertz showed that radio waves were a kind of energy, just like light, that **travelled in waves** and could be made to carry information. Many inventors were excited by this information. Marconi found that radio waves could be used to send Morse code through the air, without needing wires. In 1897, he started his own company and began to **DEVELOP HIS IDEAS** further.

Marconi's funeral in 1937 was marked by two minutes of silence on all radios across the world.

Saving lives

At first, Marconi's "*wireless telegraph*" could send signals only a few kilometres, but his waves were beaming across the Atlantic Ocean by 1901. Soon there were **transmitters on both sides of the ocean**, and wireless equipment on ships. When the *Titanic* struck an iceberg and began to sink in 1912, frantic calls for help from the radio operators onboard the ship helped to **SAVE 705 LIVES**.

It couldn't have happened without...

HEINRICH HERTZ *discovered radio waves in 1888, but he did not see their potential uses.*

NIKOLA TESLA *was the first to generate and transmit* RADIO WAVES *in 1895.*

Two magnets changed the magnetic field in the iron wire, causing it to pick up radio signals if any were present.

The magnetic detector became known as the "Maggie" by radio operators.

Radio voices

The early radios transmitted Morse code only, which was picked up by radio operators and transcribed into messages. Canadian **REGINALD FESSENDEN** made the first voice radio broadcast in 1906. The radio operators who tuned in *couldn't believe their ears* when they heard a human voice coming through for the first time. Soon, families were gathering around the radio to be entertained with **music, comedy, and drama.**

Did you know?
Radio waves can travel great distances because the Earth's upper atmosphere reflects some of them. All that is needed is a powerful transmitter and a sensitive receiver.

HOW IT WORKS

Radio technology relies on two things: the transmitter and the receiver. The transmitter turns a sound signal into a radio wave and sends it using its antenna. The receiver's antenna picks up the radio wave and turns it back into sound.

Radio wave

The receiver's antenna converts the radio waves back into sound.

The transmitter's antenna converts sound into radio waves.

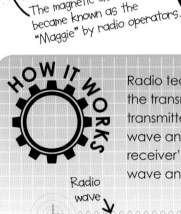

How it changed the world

The telegraph and telephone allowed people to communicate across long distances, but both needed cables, which were often difficult (and sometimes impossible) to lay. The development of radio technology meant that people could communicate directly anywhere in the world, even at sea.

It paved the way for...

We can watch **TELEVISION** thanks to radio signals, which have been transmitting television broadcasts **SINCE THE 1930s.**

MOBILE PHONES *use radio waves to communicate. The earliest mobiles date from the 1970s.*

Picture this

Pinhole cameras were used for centuries to project images, but they couldn't take a picture. Today, making snaps couldn't be easier.

Did you know?
Early daguerreotype sitters had to stay absolutely still for 60–90 seconds. No wonder most of them looked so serious!

The invention that puts you in the FRAME

Daguerreotype

The world's *first photographs* were taken by Nicéphore Niépce, but they faded quickly. Fellow Frenchman Louis-Jacques-Mandé Daguerre discovered a way of making a **permanent image** on a silver-coated copper plate. They didn't take a long time to take, and the images can still be seen today. People rushed to have their portraits immortalized on **DAGUERREOTYPES**, as they were called, in the mid-1800s.

Daguerreotype cameras developed their images on copper plates coated with a thin layer of silver.

The entire camera had to be sent to the Kodak factory to obtain the photos.

Film camera

Photography was a *complicated and time-consuming* process before American George Eastman invented roll film cameras. Eastman invented a **flexible film** to replace the glass plates that were commonly used to capture images, then, with William Walker, a roll holder for the film. His **KODAK** camera was the first to have a built-in film-roll holder when it went on sale in 1888, making photography a lot simpler.

Polaroid camera

Three-year-old Jennifer Land asked her father why a photo couldn't be seen straight after it was taken. The question led **EDWIN LAND** to invent the Polaroid camera in 1947, which worked by using chemicals inside the camera to **develop** and print the image. For the first time, people could see their photos without having to send the film away to be developed.

The photograph comes out of the front of the camera, as the image is developing.

Celluloid camera film is used by film cameras to save the picture. The film must then be developed to see the picture.

Introduced in 1909, 35mm camera film is still used today

Digital camera

Digital photography is **absolutely instant** and doesn't need film or processing. The Japanese company Sony sold the first commercial filmless camera in 1981. It used a **DISK DRIVE** to store video-camera images, but was otherwise like a normal camera. As technology got better and the cost of the components went down, the first digital cameras began to be sold. It wasn't long before almost everyone was snap-happy: digital cameras allow you to take and save as many pictures as you like, printing out only your favourites.

The screen allows you to see the image before you capture it. It also shows stored pictures.

Television

The marvellous machine that brings the WORLD to your living room

From fuzzy pictures to high-definition images, watching television has kept us informed and entertained for decades.

By the way... Some of my early inventions weren't successful: I cut myself badly with my rust-proof razor, and my air-soled shoes burst.

Baird achieved the first transatlantic TV transmission in 1928.

Baird's biscuit-tin TV

In 1926, an **excited audience** in London, England, became the first people ever to watch television. Scottish inventor **JOHN LOGIE BAIRD** had cobbled together a tea chest, biscuit tins, hat boxes, and darning needles to come up with a mechanical TV. The audience watched a scary-looking ventriloquist's dummy called *Stookie Bill*.

Switching on

Though exciting, Baird's television pictures were so **FUZZY** that his system was soon abandoned. A few years later, Russian-American inventor Vladimir Zworykin improved the ***cathode-ray tube*** (a device for showing images on a screen), and used it in a new type of electrical TV. Sales had rocketed by the 1950s, with millions of people enjoying news and entertainment via the magic of moving pictures **in their homes**.

It paved the way for...

With the invention of **VIDEOS** *and* **DVDs**, *people could watch movies at home on TV.*

Everyone could be a star after the **CAMCORDER** *was invented in 1980.*

Television enabled people to watch events happening all over the globe without leaving the house. It became the world's most popular form of entertainment.

HOW IT WORKS

In cathode-ray televisions, electron beams emerge from a cathode. Electromagnets controlled by the TV direct the electron across the screen to trace out a picture. Phosphors – substances that glow when the electron beams hit them – make the picture visible. Mixtures of red, green, and blue phosphors can make any other colour.

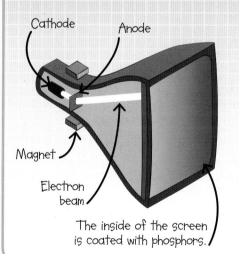

Cathode

Anode

Magnet

Electron beam

The inside of the screen is coated with phosphors.

> **Did you know?**
> Around 500 million viewers worldwide watched on TV as the first humans landed on the Moon in 1969.

Digital TV

The television you turn on today probably uses *digital technology* and a flat plasma screen instead of a cathode ray tube. Digital TV means you can choose from **LOTS MORE** TV channels, and watch your favourite programmes in great detail thanks to **high-definition image technology**.

The first **CLOSED-CIRCUIT TV** *systems were developed in the 1940s – and are now on* **MANY STREETS**.

Baird first developed **3D TV** *in 1928 – not surprisingly, it wasn't as good as the version that launched in 2010.*

Transistor

The COMPACT COMPONENT that made modern electronics possible

Vacuum tubes

Transistors are used in electronic equipment to **switch or amplify** electric signals. Before transistors, these jobs were done by vacuum tubes, which looked a bit like light bulbs, and were **unreliable and bulky**. American physicists William Shockley, Walter Brattain, and John Bardeen began developing ideas to **REPLACE** them in the 1950s.

Brattain once said "The only regret I have about the transistor is its use for rock and roll".

How it changed... the world

Transistors made electronic equipment smaller and more reliable. Without them, the gadgets we use every day wouldn't exist.

The three leads allow the transistor to stop, start, or increase electrical current.

Shockley worked for the US military during World War II.

Bardeen went on to win a second Nobel Prize for Physics in 1972.

Transistors take over

The trio's small but revolutionary solution, called the **TRANSISTOR**, could control electric current just as vacuum tubes did, but was an enormous improvement. The transistor used far less power, hardly ever failed, and was so tiny that it made it possible to have **smaller electronic equipment**. In 1956, Brattain, Bardeen, and Shockley were jointly awarded the **Nobel Prize for Physics** for their work on transistors.

Circuitry

Early transistors were about the length of the **palm of your hand**, but more improvements to their design resulted in them becoming **SMALLER**. At first, they were connected to other electronic components on circuit boards, and used in hearing aids, radios, and computers. Now, transistors are mostly found in computer chips – **hundreds of millions** of transistors can fit on a single chip.

Microchips

Early computers relied on transistors and other electrical parts connected up **by hand**. This was a laborious process, and if any one of these connections broke, the whole lot could fail. In 1958, American scientist Jack Kilby developed the integrated circuit (left). By 1961, these were a lot smaller and commonly known as **MICROCHIPS**. Each one consisted of hundreds of tiny parts, made from one piece of material (usually **silicon**). They made computer parts more reliable, organized, and consumed less power.

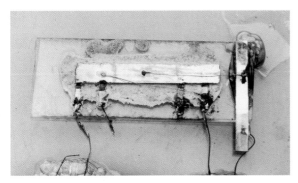

Intel labelled Hoff a "rock star" for his work on the microprocessor.

The Intel 8080 was used in the first commerical computers.

How it changed...

Without microprocessors, we wouldn't have personal computers, or any of the smart appliances that help run our lives.

the world

Mini-computer

In 1971, fellow American Ted Hoff was designing a new microchip for a scientific calculator for the company Intel. He thought it would be easier to make a chip that could be used for a **variety of functions**, as opposed to one that would work only for his calculator. His solution was the Intel 4004 microprocessor, *a mini-computer on a chip*. Further improvements led to the Intel 8080 chip, which came to be known as "the first truly usable microprocessor".

The smallest wires in today's microprocessors are less than one thousandth of the width of a human hair.

Microprocessor

The tiny technology that is the BIG BRAIN inside your computer

Chips with everything

A microprocessor is like a **BRAIN**: it reads and adds to memory, carries out instructions, and communicates with other parts of the computer. Today's microprocessors power computers, phones, washing machines, and lots more. They're thousands of times faster than the first ones, and yet they're small enough to *fit on a fingernail*.

Computer

From enormous "engines" to tiny devices that fit inside phones, computers have revolutionized our lives.

Apple's popular iMac computer was released in 1998.

The start of the INFORMATION AGE

Engines

Englishman Charles Babbage was **way ahead of his time**: he designed three computing machines in the 1820s and 1830s, which he called "**ENGINES**", though he never managed to build these huge mechanical contraptions. English mathematician Ada Lovelace devised a sequence of operations intended for Babbage's Analytical Engine to work out a maths problem – making her the first **computer programmer**.

By the way...
"Ada Lovelace Day" is celebrated in the middle of October – its goal is to encourage more girls to study the sciences.

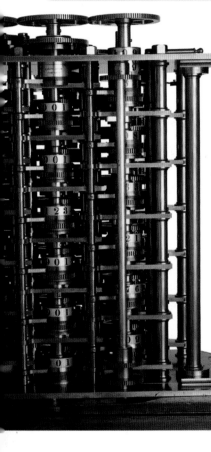

It paved the way for...

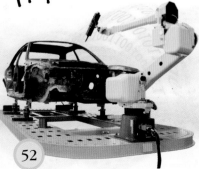

Programmed computers control **INDUSTRIAL ROBOTS,** *which do all kinds of work too difficult or dangerous for humans, such as lifting heavy loads or performing intricate tasks.*

The **INTERNET** *grew from a network of computers in the USA in the late 1960s, and the* **WORLD WIDE WEB** *brought it to the masses from the 1990s.*

Secret computers

The world's **first working computers** were both kept top secret. The first programmable computer was the Z3, invented by Konrad Zuse during World War II, and was used to make **SECRET CODES** for Germany. Britain, Germany's enemy in the war, built Colossus (right), the first digital electronic computer. Colossus enabled Britain and its allies to **break the German codes**, giving them access to top-secret German information.

Did you know?
Babbage's Difference Engine No 2 was first built in 1991, 142 years after it was designed – and it worked!

iMac

The iMac featured a computer and monitor display in one colourful case.

Apple Macintosh

The early computers were the size of **several elephants**. Transistors and then microprocessors gradually made computers smaller and cheaper, but early computer users needed skill and specialist technical knowledge.

From 1976, Americans Steve Wozniak and Steve Jobs began to change that with their **APPLE** computers, designed so that anyone could use them. Other companies soon followed, making computers cheaper, smaller, and easier to use. Soon they were in schools, offices, and homes **across the world** in technology as diverse as mobile phones, cars, and even toilets.

How it changed

Computers have revolutionized almost every part of modern life in some way – how we learn, work, and even our social lives – as they are in the things we use every day.

the world

E-READERS *have been around since 1998, but started to become popular in the 2000s, and* **TABLET COMPUTERS** *followed not long after.*

SOCIAL NETWORKING *sites have sprung up thanks to computers and the Internet. The most famous is* **FACEBOOK**, *set up in 2004 by American Mark Zuckerberg.*

Satellite

Technology that's OUT OF THIS WORLD!

Sputnik 1 was the size of a beach ball

Space tower

Russian scientist **Konstantin Tsiolkovsky** came up with the idea of building a *tower into space*, with a satellite at the top that could be used by spaceships on their way to **OTHER PLANETS**. He worked out the maths to make it happen, but his ideas never got off the ground.

By the way...
I was way ahead of my time: I wrote an equation about rockets in 1903 that's still used today!

Space Race

The world's first **satellite**, Sputnik 1, was rocketed into orbit by the USSR in 1957. The country's bitter rival, the USA, had been *developing its own satellite* and was furious to have lost the first episode of what became known as the Space Race. The first US satellite, **EXPLORER 1**, was launched just three months later.

It couldn't have happened without...

Alessandro Volta invented the world's first **BATTERY**, *the voltaic pile, in 1800.*

RADIO SIGNALS *are used to both direct satellites and receive information from them.*

Sputnik's four antennae sent information on Earth's atmosphere back to the surface.

Some satellites look like slowly moving stars

Did you know?
Laika the dog became the first animal to orbit Earth when she zoomed into space on Sputnik 2, a month after Sputnik 1.

Solar panels power the majority of satellites.

The satellite contained a battery to power it and a radio transmitter.

Modern satellites

There are now **THOUSANDS** of artificial satellites in orbit above our heads, transmitting signals or taking pictures for use in **communication, navigation, research, and even spying**. We have also sent space probes into orbit around other bodies in our Solar System: they are now satellites of the *Moon, Mercury, Venus, Mars, Jupiter, Saturn, and the Sun*.

HOW IT WORKS

Satellites use radio waves to transmit information. Communications satellites receive a radio signal beamed up to them from Earth and transmit it to another point on Earth's surface. In this way, a signal – such as a television broadcast – can be sent over a very long distance almost instantaneously.

The satellite picks up the signal, amplifies it, and sends it to dish 2.

Dish 1 sends a signal to the satellite.

Dish 2 receives the signal many kilometres away from dish 1.

How it changed the world

Satellites allow us to communicate instantly. They also warn us about wild weather, keep us from getting lost, and – experts believe – help keep the world at peace.

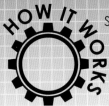

The world's first programmable **COMPUTER** *was the Z3, invented in 1941.*

The **V-2 ROCKET** *was developed by German Wernher von Braun in the* **1940s**.

Telescope

The invention and improvement of telescopes gradually revealed the distant wonders of space.

Did you know?
The Kepler Space Telescope, launched in 2009, has a mission to find other Earth-like planets beyond our Solar System.

The eye on the sky that brought the UNIVERSE into focus

Lippershey's lenses

In 1608, German-Dutch spectacle maker **Hans Lippershey** combined curved lenses in a long tube to make the **FIRST TELESCOPE**, which magnified objects up to three times. He went on to make several telescopes for the Dutch government, and was *paid very handsomely* in return.

Galileo's telescope used two lenses to make objects appear thirty times bigger.

Galileo

Italian scientist **GALILEO GALILEI** improved Lippershey's telescope in 1609 and turned it to the stars. His telescopes were able to *make distant objects appear bigger*, and gazing through them, he observed the craters of our Moon and four of Jupiter's moons, identified the fuzzy Milky Way as vast numbers of distant stars, and even realized that the **Earth orbits the Sun**.

It paved the way for...

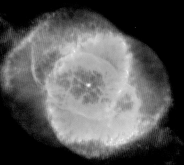

The CAT'S EYE NEBULA *is the remains of a dying star. Hubble has shown objects such as this in amazing detail.*

The two KECK TELESCOPES *in Hawaii, USA, have had their eyes on the cosmos* SINCE THE 1990s. *They observe visible light and infrared.*

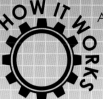

HOW IT WORKS

A refracting telescope (like Lippershey's and Galileo's) is a tube with an objective lens at one end. Light from a distant object is bent as it passes through this lens and focused into a magnified image. An eyepiece lens at the other end of the tube then magnifies the image even further. Many telescopes, including Hubble, use mirrors to help collect light – these are called reflecting telescopes.

Eye

Objective lens

Eyepiece lens

Hubble uses two precise mirrors to capture images.

Space telescopes

Since Galileo, there have been many developments in telescope technology, including the use of **MIRRORS** in telescopes to bring distant objects closer still. Perhaps the most exciting is the launching of telescopes past the blurring effects of Earth's atmosphere and into space. The most famous is the **Hubble Space Telescope**. Its 2.4-m- (8-ft-) wide main mirror has collected precious information from space, and helped us unlock some of the *secrets of the Universe*.

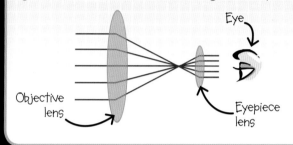

How it changed the world

Astronomy's most important invention has shown us our Solar System and beyond, and continues to help us understand how the Universe works.

Did you know?

The Hubble telescope was launched in 1990, and is still in operation, thanks to five repair missions by spacewalking astronauts.

Launched in 2003, the **Spitzer Space Telescope** detects heat energy radiated by objects in space.

The **Very Large Array** in New Mexico, USA, is a radio observatory. Its **27 antennas**, each 25 m (82 ft) across, scan the skies for radio waves.

Internet

The network that connected the world's computers, starting the INFORMATION REVOLUTION

Sharing computers

In 1969, the Advanced Research Projects Agency (ARPA) in the USA launched an **interconnected group of powerful computers**, and called it ARPANET. This novel idea enabled scientists working anywhere in the USA to share these few computers **without leaving their own place of work**. Americans Vint Cerf and Bob Kahn were two of the key experts working on the project in the 1970s.

Vint Cerf helped develop the first commercial email system.

Packet switching

ARPANET was a success and, gradually, it spread outwards to make a network of networks: what we now call the **INTERNET**. In 1973, Cerf and Kahn developed a language, called TCP/IP, to help the Internet function better. This relies on "packet switching": instead of sending data in one direction, through a central system, the data was **split into bits** (or packets). Each packet found the most efficient way across the network to its destination, where the data was **reassembled**.

If one computer server is busy, the data chooses a different route.

Computers connect to the Internet through an Internet Service Provider (ISP)'s computer.

How it changed... the world

The Internet means we always have information at our fingertips, and can share information and communicate whenever we like.

Getting connected

Along with the invention of **EMAIL** in 1972, TCP/IP allowed the Internet to really take off. It became the **standard Internet language** from 1983. Europe, via the Netherlands, became the first territory outside the USA to connect to the Internet in 1989. By this time, there were less than ten million computers connected to the Internet, but that **was about to change**.

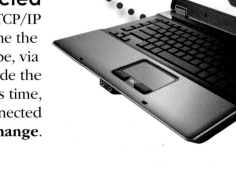

Tim Berners-Lee

The **World Wide Web** (WWW) was born at the European Organization for Nuclear Research (CERN) in Switzerland in 1990. Projects at CERN created *huge amounts of data* that scientists around the world needed to access, so English physicist Tim Berners-Lee proposed an information system for CERN that used linked documents on **WEBPAGES** accessible via the Internet.

World Wide Web

The INFORMATION-SHARING system that unlocked the Internet for millions of people

The browser bar displays the website's name, and is used to navigate the WWW.

Spreading the word

The world's **first website** was set up by Tim Berners-Lee at CERN in 1990. The site showed how people could build their own websites, and Berners-Lee and his colleagues sent out software and spread the word as widely as they could, so that *more sites soon appeared*. As time has passed, websites have become more **SOPHISTICATED**, containing pictures, videos, sound, adverts, and more.

Hyperlinks, such as this advert, take you to a new webpage.

How it changed...

Almost everyone accesses the Internet via the World Wide Web, which has made it easier than ever to send and receive information.

the world

Free for all

CERN made the source code for the World Wide Web software available to everyone **free of charge**. Even today, anyone can run a website, and access the web, for nothing. Making the technology freely available was the *key to its success*. By 1993 the WWW was doubling in size every three months – there are more than **250 MILLION** websites on the WWW today.

convenience

How many times a day do you press a button or flick a switch? With great gadgets and gizmos created to save us hours and effort, you have an instant helping hand for almost any task. We've got used to telling the time in a second, choosing a spin cycle to clean clothes, or bringing a new toy to life with a couple of batteries. Thanks to some clever people's light bulb moments, these creature comforts are now a reality, bringing quick fixes we can't live without.

Flushing

You might take toilets for granted, but life-saving loos aren't just a public convenience.

toilet

The user lifts the D-shaped handle to open the water supply and flush the pan.

More than just a FLUSH in the pan

Ancient toilets

Early toilets were basically **open-air holes** in the ground, such as this Roman lavatory from the 2nd century CE. Over the centuries, **SEWAGE SYSTEMS** developed for waste to flow into and be carried away. There were simple forms of the flush toilet in many **ancient civilizations**, including in China, Egypt, Persia (modern-day Iran), and Greece.

Royal flush

Centuries passed and **chamber pots** were all the rage. A pot was placed under the bed for regular use, with the smelly contents often chucked out of the window! **JOHN HARRINGTON**, godson to Queen Elizabeth I of England, invented a more advanced flushing loo in the 1590s, which let water out of a tank and down a pipe to clean the bowl. He installed one for **the Queen**, who wasn't impressed, and the invention didn't catch on.

By the way... I wrote a book full of toilet humour about my invention. My godmother, the Queen, was so upset she banished me!

It paved the way for...

The first **TOILET PAPER** went on sale in 1857, though the earliest use was probably in China during the 14th century.

The first **PUBLIC LAVATORY** with flushing toilets opened in London in the **1850s**. Today's public toilets are separate cubicles with locks and often a fee for use.

Going round the bend

Deadly diseases, including cholera and typhoid, were **spread** because waste wasn't flushed away. In 1775, Scottish inventor **ALEXANDER CUMMINGS** came to the rescue with his toilet. His invention was an improvement on previous loos because the pipe that took away the waste included an **S trap**, a double bend that stopped horrible whiffs from finding their way back up the pipe. The toilet was a relief to everyone and his design became the prototype for future toilets.

Like Cummings' toilet, modern toilets still use a bend to trap water, usually in a U-shape. There have been some improvements, but the basic flushing toilet design has stayed the same, whooshing water down a pipe to carry waste away.

Water from the cistern flushes the bowl when the handle is pulled.

Flushed waste travels along a drain to join main sewers.

Bend traps water, which stops smells coming up from the sewers.

The average person spends three years on the toilet!

Invented in 1870 by Stevens Hellyer, the Optimus was an advanced toilet design, with an under-the-rim flushing mechanism that was much more effective than previous versions.

Did you know?
Before toilet paper, people used moss or leaves. Rich people might have used cloth, such as wool or even lace.

How it changed

Diseases caused by sewage can kill. The flushing toilet has done more to stop the spread of these diseases than any other invention – flushing loos have saved millions of lives.

the world

CARBOLIC SOAP

Toilets cleaned up their act with the arrival of **DISINFECTANTS**. Carbolic acid was in use from the 1860s to kill germs and improve cleanliness.

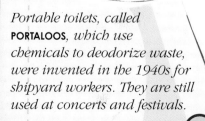

Portable toilets, called **PORTALOOS**, which use chemicals to deodorize waste, were invented in the 1940s for shipyard workers. They are still used at concerts and festivals.

Pendulum clock

Timekeeping in the past was often hit and miss. The invention of the pendulum clock ensured things ran like clockwork.

Keeping the world ON TIME

Precise pendulums

Italian inventor **GALILEO GALILEI** realized that the regular swing of a **pendulum** was a good way to measure time, but it was Dutch mathematician **CHRISTIAAN HUYGENS** who started clocks ticking with precision. His pendulum clock of 1656 counted the seconds *much more accurately* than previous weight-driven clocks. It was so reliable that Huygens fitted his clock with a **second hand** as well as minute and hour hands.

Sundials used the Sun's position in the sky to tell the time.

Early clocks

People have always tried to keep track of the time. More than 9,000 years ago people used **SUNDIALS**. In ancient Egypt and Babylon (modern-day Iraq) the **constant drip of water** was used to measure time. Mechanical clocks were invented in the 1300s, driven by *falling weights*, but they did not measure time accurately.

By the way...
As well as inventing the most accurate clock in the world, I built a telescope and discovered the rings of the planet Saturn.

It paved the way for...

From about the **1500s**, POCKET WATCHES *were carried by the wealthy though they weren't very accurate at first.*

Scottish clock-maker Alexander Bain invented the first ELECTRIC CLOCK in **1840**.

HOW IT WORKS The time a pendulum takes to swing back and forth is always the same, as long as the length of the pendulum doesn't change and it keeps swinging. In a pendulum clock, the regular swing of the pendulum is captured by the escapement. The escapement is a device that uses the energy of the regular swing of the pendulum to allow the falling weight to move the hands on the clock face. At the same time, the escapement transfers energy from a falling weight to the pendulum to keep it swinging.

Escapement

For each swing of the pendulum, one tooth of the escapement wheel is released.

Weight falls under the pull of gravity and makes the escapement wheel turn.

Pendulum

Marine chronometer

Pendulum clocks kept time on land, but at sea they were useless because of the repeated rocking of ships on the waves. Since **NAVIGATION** depended on telling the time accurately, and could mean the difference between a successful voyage and a shipping disaster, governments offered a fortune in prize money to anyone who invented an accurate clock **without a pendulum**. In 1762, English carpenter **JOHN HARRISON** won the British government's prize with his *Number Four marine chronometer*.

Did you know? Captain Cook relied on Harrison's marine chronometer during his 1772 voyage from the Tropics to Antarctica.

Huygens' clock was the template for all pendulum clocks that followed. It used a falling weight to make the pendulum swing.

Marine chronometers used a balance wheel and a spring instead of a pendulum.

How it changed the world

Pendulum clocks remained the world's most accurate clocks for 300 years. Measuring time accurately not only meant that everyone could keep time, but also gave science an essential tool for experiments and research.

QUARTZ CRYSTALS, *which vibrate at a constant rate in an electrical circuit, were first used in clocks in* **1927**.

ATOMIC CLOCKS *are the most precise timekeepers in the world. The first accurate one was made in* **1955** *by English physicist Louis Essen.*

Light bulb

The invention that LIT UP the world

From the beginning of the dimly-lit 1800s, inventors groped about for ways to turn electricity into light.

Davy's lamp was designed to help miners, as an alternative to fire, which could cause accidents.

Joseph Swan's house, in Gateshead, England, was the first ever to be lit by a light bulb.

Longer lasting tungsten filaments were invented in 1910.

Switching on

The first **electric light** was switched on by Humphry Davy when he connected two charcoal rods to a battery in 1809. Davy's light was bright, but it didn't last long. It showed that *some materials glow* when electricity passes through them, but the lights often caught fire. Fellow Englishman Joseph Swan experimented with removing the **AIR** from the bulb in the 1870s to stop this, but ran into other problems.

Did you know?
The first buildings with electric light had warning notices in them advising people not to light the bulbs with a match.

It paved the way for...

The first **CAR HEADLAMPS** *used oil, but much safer* **ELECTRIC** *ones were invented in 1898.*

Neon lights, which contain the gas **NEON**, *were invented by Frenchman* **GEORGES CLAUDE** *in 1910.*

Edison's light-bulb moment

Meanwhile, in the USA, **Thomas Edison** was experimenting with light bulbs too. He realized that the **FILAMENT** – the bit that gets hot and glows – was the key to long-lasting light. By 1880, his charred bamboo filaments were burning for more than 1,200 hours. After falling out over who invented what, **Edison and Swan joined forces**. Soon after, they were bringing light to everybody.

By the way...
I carried out 4,700 experiments with different materials to find the perfect filament, including hair from a beard.

Thomas Edison said "we will make electricty so cheap that only the rich will burn candles".

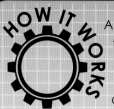

HOW IT WORKS

A light bulb's filament is made out of material that does not conduct electricity very well. This resistance to the current makes the filament heat up and radiate light. The bulb is filled with non-reactive gases so that the hot filament does not catch fire.

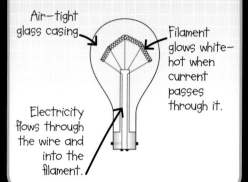

Air-tight glass casing

Filament glows white-hot when current passes through it.

Electricity flows through the wire and into the filament.

Plugging in

POWER STATIONS were set up so electricity could reach everybody with Edison's bulbs. The first ever *electricity company* started off with 52 customers in 1882. Before long, people were finding their way home in the dark by the light of **electric streetlamps**, and flicking switches for lights in their homes. This advert for Edison's bulbs dates from 1909.

How it changed

Light bulbs meant safe, bright lighting at the flick of a switch. Only now, after more than a hundred years, is the basic design being improved to make it more efficient.

the world

FLASH BULBS *were invented in 1929, replacing dangerous and noisy* **FLASH POWDER**.

The first practical **LIGHT-EMITTING DIODE** *(LED) was developed in 1962. They can be used as a replacement for light bulbs.*

Home helpers

Not so long ago, cleaning and cooking were time-consuming, boring jobs. These clever devices lend a hand around the home so we can spend our time in more interesting ways.

The APPLIANCE of science

Washing machine

Imagine having to wash and dry your clothes **BY HAND**. The first domestic washing machines took some of the strain but were hand-powered, while enormous, clanking, steam-powered washing machines operated in businesses. Finally, **electric washing machines** were invented in the early 20th century – one of the first was invented by American *Alva Fisher* in 1908. This Canadian version dates from around 1920.

Vacuum cleaner

From 1901, British engineer **Hubert Cecil Booth** offered vacuum cleaning to rich Londoners with his huge **HORSE-DRAWN**, petrol-driven machine, from which a long hose would snake into the house through a window. *James Spangler*, a janitor in a US department store, invented a much smaller electric vacuum cleaner in 1907. He started a business that later became the Hoover Company.

Can opener

After canned food was invented in 1812, there was a long wait to open it safely. Canned army rations had instructions to use a **HAMMER AND CHISEL**. People bashed and gouged away until 1870, when American inventor *William Lyman* patented a can opener with a cutting wheel. In the 1920s, safer rotary can openers were invented, based on Lyman's design.

This dishwasher from 1921 connected to a hot tap via a hose attachment.

Dishwasher

By the 1800s, American women were **FED UP** with doing the dishes. More than 30 of them came up with machines to take on the dull task, but the first successful one was invented by socialite **Josephine Cochran** in 1886, who wanted to find a way to stop her china being chipped by heavy-handed servants. Her machines were *hand-powered* for use at home, but bigger *steam-powered* ones were installed in hotels and restaurants.

Microwave oven

These handy food heaters were invented during World War II, after American radar scientist **Percy LeBaron Spencer** noticed that the microwave-producing radar set he was using had *melted his chocolate bar*. He realized the machine's potential for **COOKING FOOD**, and the first commercial microwave ovens went on sale in 1947.

This Philips microwave oven dates from the 1960s.

Refrigerator

From hauling chunks of ice down mountains to opening a fridge door, chilling out has become a lot easier.

In early refrigerators the compressor unit was found on top of the unit. Now it is hidden inside.

The COOLEST invention of them all

The big freeze

Before fridges, people kept food from spoiling by storing it in **cool, dark places** or in a **hole packed with ice or snow** brought from the nearest mountain or frozen lake. Later on, rich families had purpose-built **ICEHOUSES**, with ice often imported in blocks from **overseas**. The trade in ice continued into the 1950s – this iceman is supplying ice to businesses from his truck.

First fridges

In 1748, Scottish physician **William Cullen** discovered that evaporating ether could create freezing temperatures, because evaporating liquids absorb heat. The first chilling machine, invented by American engineer **Jacob Perkins** in 1834, used this principle. Soon, **INDUSTRIAL FRIDGES** were cooling beer and meat. Domestic fridges became available in the 20th century.

Did you know?
In 1841, American doctor John Gorrie invented a fridge to cool feverish patients. It was the forerunner of air conditioning.

Several shelves stored food and there was a small compartment for ice.

It paved the way for...

Refrigeration units for **COOLER TRUCKS** were used from the 1930s, making perishable goods much **EASIER TO TRANSPORT**.

First introduced into shops in the 1870s, **CHILLER CABINETS** kept food **FRESHER FOR LONGER**.

General Electric made and sold this affordable steel fridge from 1927, finally making the fridge a common household appliance.

Fatal fridges

Until 1929 fridges were deadly – they used **poisonous gases** as coolants and were responsible for several deaths. As a result, a safer **CHLOROFLUOROCARBON (CFC)** called freon was used to cool refrigerators. It was not harmful to human health, but later scientists realized that CFCs were destroying the Earth's ozone layer. Modern fridges use *a less harmful coolant* to reduce the environmental impact. They can also be recycled safely.

HOW IT WORKS

A refrigerator works by changing a substance called a coolant from a liquid to a gas, and back. The liquid passes through an expansion valve, which turns it into a cold gas. The gas absorbs heat from the refrigerator's contents, keeping them cool. The gas is compressed into a liquid as it leaves the refrigerator, which heats it up. The liquid loses heat to the room before passing through the expansion valve again.

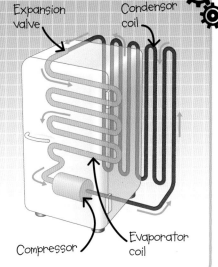

Expansion valve

Condensor coil

Compressor

Evaporator coil

Did you know?
German physicist Albert Einstein invented a fridge in partnership with former student Leo Szilard and patented it in 1930.

How it changed

Chilling food keeps food fresher and safer for longer. This has changed customer shopping habits – people no longer have to go shopping every day, saving time and effort.

the world

American Clarence Birdseye *invented a method of* FLASH FREEZING *food in 1929, and not long afterwards* DOMESTIC FREEZERS *became popular.*

The first large-scale AIR-CONDITIONING UNIT *was invented in 1902 by American inventor* **WILLIS HAVILAND CARRIER**. *It used the same principle as the fridge.*

Plastic

Try getting through a day without touching something made of plastic. This flexible friend can be moulded into shape, and then sets solid. It is used to make many of the things we use every day.

By the way...
As well as Bakelite, I also patented about fifty other inventions, including types of electric insulation, synthetic resin, and photographic paper.

The MOULDABLE MATERIAL that shaped the world

Leo Baekeland received the US patent for his invention in 1909.

Bakelite was heat-proof and did not conduct electricity.

Fantastic plastic

People have used *natural materials*, such as **rubber** and **tortoiseshell**, for thousands of years, shaping them into hard-wearing objects. In 1905, Belgian-born chemist **LEO BAEKELAND** mixed phenol (a disinfectant) with formaldehyde (a preservative) and came up with Bakelite, *the first completely human-made plastic*. This versatile material can be moulded into shape but sets hard and doesn't melt easily. It was used to make music records, furniture, jewellery, and this radio cover.

It couldn't have happened without...

In about **1600** BCE, people in Mesoamerica played games with **RUBBER BALLS** made from latex – a natural plastic found in rubber trees.

American **CHARLES GOODYEAR** invented vulcanization in 1839, which made rubber stretchy but also able to **BOUNCE BACK INTO SHAPE**.

Plenty of plastic

Bakelite **proved so handy** that chemists rushed to make new and even more useful plastics. In the 1930s, American chemist **WALLACE CAROTHERS** produced the *first completely human-made fibre*, nylon. In the same decade newly invented Perspex was taking the place of glass and polythene began to be used in packaging. Soon plastics were finding more and more uses.

Nylon stockings became a popular replacement for silk during the 1940s. →

HOW IT WORKS

Plastics are polymers – materials made of molecules that consist of thousands or millions of atoms. Polymers are made by joining together small molecules (monomers) in a repeating structure that forms very long chains. Many different molecules can be used, and combined in a variety of different ways – this is why there is such a variety of types of plastic.

Ethene molecule (monomer)

Several ethene molecules join together to form polythene (a common type of plastic).

Going green

Today plastic is everywhere – from the packaging of your food to the **RUBBER DUCK** in your bathtub. Most plastics are produced from oil, *a limited resource*, and can takes centuries to rot down once discarded. **Bioplastics** made from organic material are now being developed as a **GREEN ALTERNATIVE** to oil-based plastics.

How it changed the world

Plastic is lightweight, cheap, tough, difficult to break, and doesn't rot. No wonder it's absolutely everywhere: in packaging, toys, furniture, computers, and clothing. But because it doesn't rot, rubbish tips are full of plastic that will take hundreds of years to break down.

English inventor **ALEXANDER PARKES** *made a semi-synthetic plastic called* **PARKESINE** *in 1856, used to make a variety of domestic objects.*

Battery

Today batteries are useful if you can't plug a device into an outlet, but when they were first invented, they were the only things capable of generating an electric current.

The invention that ELECTRIFIED the planet

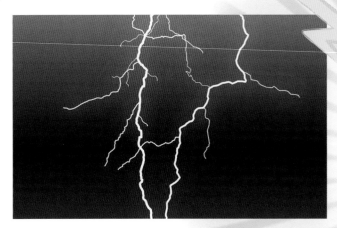

In Galvani's experiment, the frog was the equivalent of the brine-soaked paper in Volta's pile.

Electrical storm

Electricity is as old as lightning. In 1752, American scientist **BENJAMIN FRANKLIN** flew a kite with a metal key in a storm and realized that sparks coming from the metal proved that lightning is a *form of electricity*. This static ("at rest") electricity was first discovered in ancient Greece by a mathematician named Thales who produced a **static electric charge** by polishing amber with animal fur.

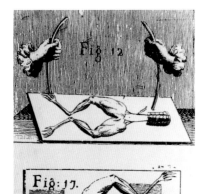

Frog findings

Even though people knew about electricity, they did not yet know how to produce an electric current – a flow of electric charge. In 1780, Italian doctor **LUIGI GALVANI** noticed that the muscles in the legs of dead frogs twitched when they made contact with two different metals. He thought this was caused by "*animal electricity*" in the frog itself. But fellow scientist **ALESSANDRO VOLTA** realized that the electricity wasn't due to the dead frog, but to the different metals.

Did you know?
French emperor Napoleon I was so impressed with Alessandro Volta's invention of the voltaic pile that he made him a count.

It paved the way for...

*Understanding current electricity led to the **ELECTRICITY SUPPLY** we have come to rely on today. The first public electricity supply lit the streets of Godalming, UK, in **1881**.*

Voltaic pile

Volta had discovered that two different metals submerged in acid could **generate a tiny electric current** between them. In 1800, he created his *voltaic pile* – the world's first ever battery. It was made from layers of copper, cardboard soaked in saltwater, and zinc – each group of three makes a "cell", and *the more cells* the greater the electric current produced. The current is generated by a **CHEMICAL REACTION** that moves electrons from one metal to the other.

Zinc disc

Saltwater-soaked cardboard

Copper disc

By the way...
It took me years of experimentation before I discovered the first practical method of generating electricity. The unit "volt" is named after me.

Charging ahead

The voltaic pile was groundbreaking, but it leaked and didn't last long. The first **RECHARGEABLE** battery was the *lead-acid battery* invented in 1859 by French physicist Gaston Planté. The basic principle of this version remained unchanged into the 21st century. The first **dry battery** (using paste instead of liquid) was the zinc-carbon one created by German scientist **CARL GASSNER** in 1886, which led to the convenient batteries we slot into torches today.

How it changed the world

The battery was the first means of generating an electric current and the first easily portable energy source. Without it there would be no phones, radio, or battery-operated devices.

Volta also discovered methane gas while poking about in a marsh and invented an exploding pistol that he used to work out the oxygen content of air.

*The **ELECTRIC TORCH** first came into use in 1899. Like today's torches, it used a dry cell battery.*

*Tablet computers, **MOBILE PHONES**, and other mobile devices in everyday use all depend on a battery as a power source.*

Hook and eye

People have been **HOOKING UP** their clothes for hundreds of years. In the 1300s, hook-and-eye fasteners were known as "crochet and loop" ("crochet" is French for "hook"), and the *simple yet effective* design hasn't changed much ever since. Hook-and-eye fastenings lent their support to the **world's first brassieres**, or bras, which were invented in the 1400s. Most of today's bras still use them.

Safety pin

Brooches were used to fasten clothes more than a thousand years before the invention of the safety pin in 1849. American inventor Walter Hunt's design *improved on the brooch*: it was made from a single piece of wire, for easy manufacture, it used a coil in the wire rather than a hinge, and the clasp fastened the pin and shielded the user's fingers at the same time. It was **SIMPLE, YET BRILLIANT**.

Keeping it together

Everything would fall apart without the help of these small but useful inventions.

The most important part of your WARDROBE

The zip is the world's most widely used fastener

A zip's teeth are brought together and locked into place by the slider.

Snap fastener

If you were an actor with a *quick change* between scenes in the 1800s, you might use some of these newly invented fasteners, which made whipping costumes **on and off** easy. German Heribert Bauer's 1885 snap fastener was improved by American Jack Weil during the 1900s, who added them to denim shirts in place of buttons – the finishing touch to the **COWBOY LOOK**.

Zip

American Whitcomb Judson wanted to get his **BOOTS** on and off quicker, so in 1893 he invented a fastener that hooked them up with one pull, using a sliding device on a row of clasps. Judson's fastener tended to come undone, but *Gideon Sundback* developed a version that used metal teeth on flexible tape. It was used as the fastener for a boot called the Zipper, and **the name stuck**.

Velcro®

George de Mestral got the idea for Velcro® when he saw burdock burrs sticking to his dog's coat. When he looked at them through a microscope, he saw that the burrs were covered in tiny hooks that attached to loops in the dog's fur. He developed **VELCRO®** so that one side is covered in tiny hooks, and the other in tiny loops. The name comes from the French *"velours croché"*, or "hooked velvet".

Velcro® works like microscopic hooks and eyes

77

Work and play

Time is money in our busy world, so great inventions that reduce workloads and improve productivity are always welcomed. From robots to barcodes, inspiring ideas have revolutionized business, raking in megabucks. That's all in a day's work, but what about letting off some steam afterwards? Brilliant breakthroughs in the entertainment and leisure industries have stolen the limelight, allowing us to kick back and enjoy our free time.

Money

Though made of only cheap metals or paper, money makes it easier to BUY the things you need

Coining it in

Before money, people would swap or **BARTER** for the things they needed. Over time, useful or beautiful things, such as shells, feathers, and *even dried tea*, were used instead of bartering. In about 650 BCE, the kingdom of Lydia (modern-day western Turkey) began to stamp gold and silver metal discs called staters (above). They were the **first coins**.

Making notes

Paper money took shape in China by the 1100s, as a way of avoiding the weighty coinage necessary to *complete large transactions*. Though news of printed money filtered into Europe, it was another 500 years before **SWEDEN** issued the continent's first banknotes in 1661.

How it changed...
Money has transformed the world into a global economy made up of different currencies, giving almost everything a price. **the world**

The chip stores information about the account.

Cash to credit

These days, most people **splash their cash** without using coins or banknotes at all. **SMARTCARDS** enable you to access the money in your bank account at any time. Banks also issue *credit cards*, allowing consumers to buy items immediately and pay back the debts over time.

4321 9876 5012 9900
2012
10/12
10/20

Sand solution

When American student **Joseph Woodland** was researching a technology that could identify food products in 1948, he found the solution on a **BEACH**. As he drew lines in the sand with his fingers, he thought of a code of bars and spaces. This resulted in the Universal Product Code (UPC), or barcode system, which was first adopted in 1974 and **continues to be in use today**.

Barcode

It revolutionized retail and is the best system for RECOGNIZING objects, bar none

Black and white bars of different widths represent a number from 1–9.

A laser scans the bars for a computer to read.

Guard bars are longer and separate the two codes.

The six-digit manufacturing code identifies the maker of the product.

Product code (last six digits) is unique to the item being sold.

9 781405 391450

Code conversion

Barcodes are basically *identity tags*. At a glance, they are a series of vertical bars of different widths on a product's packaging. When read by a **LASER SCANNER**, the item is quickly identified together with information about it, such as price and stock information. About **five billion** bar codes are scanned every day.

Plough
THIS ICON OF AGRICULTURE remains top of the crops for farmers

The plough is a farming tool used to prepare the earth for the seed-sowing season. Ploughing has saved farmers' time and toil in the fields, and transformed food production.

Did you know?
Camels and llamas have been used to pull ploughs in regions where there were too few horses and oxen.

The handle is held and steered by the farmer.

Ancient ards

Ploughing has been an integral part of the **FARMING CALENDAR** since ancient times. Turning the earth in the autumn prepares the ground for seed sowing in the spring. In about **5000 BCE** early civilizations broke the ground with an **antler or branch** to cultivate crops. This developed into a pointed wooden plough called an **ARD**. The ancient Egyptians attached the ard to a beam harnessed to two oxen and set to work ploughing the Nile valley.

Cast-iron progress

During the **1800s** the design of the plough improved when the wooden point was flattened into a **blade of iron**. Called a share, this blade sliced into the ground, loosening and turning the soil. The result was a neat strip of soil, or **FURROW**, running through the land. The plough pioneered the **Agricultural Revolution**, reducing the effort required to produce plenty more crops. Metal blades are still used to cut furrows today.

By the way...
Medieval ploughs were so heavy that it was not uncommon for eight oxen to pull a single machine.

Share blade cuts and loosens soil.

It paved the way for...

*In 1700, Englishman **JETHRO TULL** invented the **SEED DRILL**. This device dropped seeds down a chute into a furrow in organized rows called drills.*

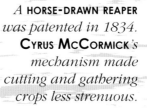

*A **HORSE-DRAWN REAPER** was patented in 1834. **CYRUS MCCORMICK**'s mechanism made cutting and gathering crops less strenuous.*

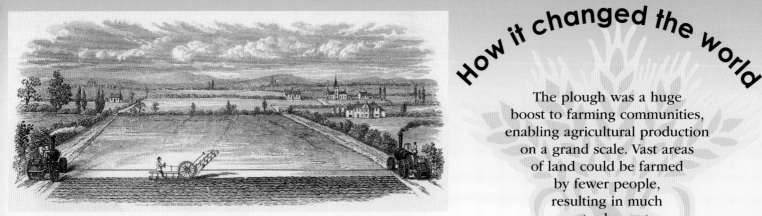

The plough was a huge boost to farming communities, enabling agricultural production on a grand scale. Vast areas of land could be farmed by fewer people, resulting in much greater harvests.

Steam-powered ploughs

By the 1860s, the **invention of the steam engine** made animals second choice for pulling ploughs. English engineer **JOHN FOWLER** devised the ***double-engine system***, which put steam engines at both sides of a field pulling "anti-balance" ploughs on a steel rope. These **tipped at each end** so the land could be ploughed back and forth, producing **SIX FURROWS** at a time. Fowler's ploughs were exported to Europe and Africa, but the expense meant only large farms used them.

Beam is attached to an animal or vehicle.

Turning the soil makes it more fertile and buries weeds so they can break down.

Today TRACTORS *pull along large metal ploughs. Though this* HEAVY-DUTY MACHINERY *does the hard work, the basic principle remains the same.*

The benefits of ploughing led to CROP ROTATION *to ensure fertile soil and bountiful harvests. Rapid food production led to* INDUSTRIAL-SCALE FARMING.

Crane

Heavy loads are given a LIFT by an invention that's happy to do all the hard work

Early cranes

Invented in **ANCIENT GREECE** in about **515** BCE, the crane was adopted and developed further by the Romans. Early Roman cranes used *treadmills powered by slaves*. These machines made it easier to handle and lift building materials and other **heavyweight items**.

The pulley – a rope wrapped around a wheel with a groove in it – is the key to a crane's lifting power.

A

Rope loops over the top pulley, so the rope is pulled down but the load is lifted vertically.

A

B

Slaves walking inside the treadmill turn the wheel, which pulls on the rope to lift the load.

Two pulleys connected by a rope are known as a compound pulley.

B

A compound pulley shares the weight of the load between two pulleys, so less lifting force is required.

How it changed... Cranes have taken the weight off workers' shoulders, carrying heavy loads and helping to construct tall buildings that redefine city skylines. **the world**

Modern cranes

Today's cranes are **crafted from steel** and run on engines or electric motors. Tower cranes are used by construction workers to lift the **HEAVY LOADS** involved in erecting tall buildings. Other cranes carry *weighty containers* on board ships or move objects around factories.

Explosive mix

Italian chemist *Ascanio Sobrero* discovered **LIQUID NITROGLYCERIN** in 1847, but this explosive was so dangerous that even a knock could set it off. The **hazardous nature** of nitroglycerin made it impossible to use. Explosives needed to become *more stable* if they were ever to be beneficial.

Dynamite

A truly EXPLOSIVE invention originally intended to put safety first

How it changed...

Dynamite transformed the construction industry, clearing the way for railways and roads and blasting tunnels through rock.

the world

3. BANG! The shock from the exploding blasting cap makes the dynamite itself explode.

BOOM!

Off with a bang!

After studying chemical engineering, Swedish scientist *Alfred Nobel* was determined to make more stable explosives. He found that mixing nitroglycerin with **KIESELGUHR** (a chalky sand) resulted in a safe explosive that could be dropped without exploding and yet **detonated on demand** with a blasting cap. He called his invention "**DYNAMITE**".

2. The blasting cap, a small explosive device attached to the dynamite, is set off by the current.

Promise of peace

Nobel believed dynamite would *aid the construction* of roads, tunnels, and mines. However, to his disappointment, dynamite also became a **weapon of war**, so Nobel left his fortune to establish the **NOBEL PRIZE**. Since 1901, this annual set of awards recognizes the work that most helps humankind.

1. When the plunger is pushed into the blasting box, an electric current travels down the wire to the blasting cap.

NAT. MDCCC XXXIII OB. MDCCC XCVI

ALFR. NOBEL

Portland cement

Early civilizations relied on **natural minerals** to bond building materials together. By the 19th century, factories made basic cement from **local limestone and clay**. In 1824, British bricklayer **JOSEPH ASPDIN** ground cooked limestone and clay into powder and **added water**. He named the strong concrete Portland cement after quality Portland stone. **AFFORDABLE AND HARDWEARING**, cement is used to lay bricks, plaster walls, and construct roads.

Steel

Steel is an alloy (mixture) of iron and other substances. It has been used for **thousands of years**, but it really took off in 1858 when Englishman **Henry Bessemer** invented a process to produce large amounts of it very cheaply. In 1913, English laboratory researcher **Harry Brearley** was in pursuit of a long-lasting steel for gun barrels, when he discovered a type that **resisted damage** from acids. Today his **STAINLESS STEEL** is everywhere, from items such as saucepans and sinks to tiny nuts and bolts holding household goods together.

Strong steel girders are used in construction to form the supporting structure of buildings.

Material world

People have been crafting objects since ancient times, but these marvellous materials have transformed the way we live.

Did you know?
The ancient Romans used volcano ash to make their concrete. Today, about 1.2 billion tonnes of cement is produced every year.

The materials that BUILT the modern world

Glass

Heating the mineral sodium carbonate and sand produces glass, but it is unclear who discovered the process. The Egyptians were **glazing jewellery beads** from 2500 BCE, while the ancient Romans were first to use transparent glass. In about **1000** CE, the glass industry took off in Europe, with **THE VENETIANS OF ITALY** producing the finest glass for centuries afterwards. By the 17th century, most Europeans had glass **windowpanes** at home. Spectacles, mirrors, and light bulbs are among the many inventions that make use of glass.

Stainless steel is often used for hand tools

Did you know?
The windows of protected vehicles, such as tanks and military aircraft, have such thick layers of glass that they could stop a bullet.

Kevlar® makes these work gloves cut-proof

Kevlar®

This **synthetic fibre** is a relatively young invention in the material world. Created by American chemist **STEPHANIE KWOLEK** and patented in 1966, Kevlar® is five times stronger than steel. In addition to **super strength**, it is lightweight and does not rust. This makes the tightly woven fibres ideal for **BULLETPROOF VESTS** worn by police officers. As well as saving lives, Kevlar® is used to make parachutes, skis, mobile phones, construction clothing, bicycle tyres, and **underwater cables**.

Titanium

In 1791, English clergyman **William Gregor** discovered titanium in its mineral form, but it wasn't until 1932 that Luxembourg metal expert William Kroll produced the **METALLIC TITANIUM** used today. Removing impurities leaves a material **as strong as steel but half as heavy**. Named after the Titans of Greek mythology, titanium makes aircraft, spacecraft, boats, bicycles, and machine parts like these cogs.

Robot

Once they existed only as science fiction, but today's robots are indispensible workers in factories across the world.

The WIRED-UP WORKER who never gets sick or tired

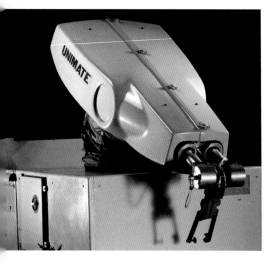

Unimate

The first real robot, called Unimate, was a **computerized robotic arm** with a gripper attached. In 1961, US car manufacturer **GENERAL MOTORS** became the first company to use a Unimate robot in its production process. Unimate welded parts, poured liquid metal, and stacked metal sheets.

Hard at work

Unimate led the way for *robotic employees*, with more than one million robots at work in industry today. In the car industry, robots are now in the driving seat, making up **ONE IN EVERY 10** car production workers. Their robotic arms have been developed so a **variety of tools** can be attached, such as hooks, grippers, or welding equipment.

It paved the way for...

SURGICAL ROBOTS *with arms and viewers called endoscopes allow surgeons to perform operations with far greater* PRECISION *than they could by hand.*

Help in the home could soon come from ROBOT HOUSEKEEPERS. *PaPePo robots* ASSIST WITH CHORES, *control household devices, and monitor emails.*

Ideal applicants

For an employer, a robot is the perfect employee. It works fast and performs **REPETITIVE TASKS** but never tires or makes mistakes. Dangerous tasks such as **clearing landmines** or **putting out fires** are no problem to a robot without feeling. Put in a dark, hot, or unpleasant place, robots work without complaint or payment.

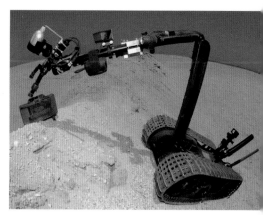

Artificial intelligence

Robots do not have the natural intelligence of people. Jobs requiring *decision-making* are better suited to people. Developing artificial intelligence is the focus for robotic engineers today. Some robots already recognize faces, play instruments, and detect smells. This robot, called **KISMET**, was developed by US researcher Cynthia Breazeal in the 1990s to show how humans and robots can interact.

How it changed the world

To date, robots have been used mainly as slave labour, doing the dirty work that people want to avoid. This has cut costs and increased production. But with advances in artificial intelligence, who knows what this incredible invention will be capable of in the future?

For those who want a ready-trained animal friend, **ROBOT PETS** *could be the answer. Robot dogs and cats move like real animals, but they also* **SING AND DANCE***!*

Busy hospitals and care homes may soon use **ROBOT NURSES** *to assist with care.* **LIFTING AND CARRYING** *patients is one task that robots carry out with ease.*

Desk buddies

Space-saving scribblers, handy adhesives, and innovative organizers make great desk buddies in schools and offices around the world.

The essentials for keeping you ORGANIZED

Lead pencil

Though the **Babylonians and Egyptians** were inscribing stones and tablets thousands of years ago, it was not until the late 18th century that lead pencils first made their mark. The forerunner to the lead pencil that we use today was invented in *France and Austria* during the 1790s. Erasers were added to the end of pencils in the 1850s. Today, more than **14 BILLION** pencils are manufactured annually.

Ballpoint pen

Early ink pens proved problematic because often the ink inside either *dried up or leaked*. In the 1880s, American John J Loud developed an early version of the ballpoint pen, which was later improved by Hungarian journalist **LÁSZLÓ BÍRÓ** in the 1940s. A tiny, rotating metal ball added to a tube of ink controlled the flow and prevented drying. More than **100 billion** ballpoint pens have been sold since.

⇦ *Before the rubber eraser was invented, bread was used to remove pencil marks*

Post-it note

Created by American company 3M, the **POST-IT NOTE** allows you to attach notes to most surfaces without leaving a mark. *The same note can be used repeatedly* as only some of the glue bubbles on the adhesive strip pop each time. The Post-it went on sale in the USA in 1980 before **going global**.

⇦ The world's largest paperclip stood 9 m (30 ft) in height

Pocket calculator

The early equivalent of the calculator was a counting device called an **abacus**. Mechanical calculators developed over time, *but something didn't add up*: they were slow, bulky machines, operated by hand cranks. American company Texas Instruments developed the first handheld calculator in 1967. By the 1970s, calculators were pocket-sized – **GREAT GIZMOS** for number-crunching school pupils and office workers.

Every year, more than six million rolls of sticky tape are sold just before Christmas

Sticky tape

Another employee of 3M, Richard Drew, developed **sticky tape** in 1930 after researching adhesives and the material cellophane. The transparent tape coincided with a huge **ECONOMIC DOWNTURN** in the USA. Consumers welcomed a product that *fixed their household* goods when new ones were unaffordable.

Back to basics

In the late 1800s, miners, farmers, and factory workers in the USA found their demanding jobs required **resilient clothing**. American tailor Jacob Davis strengthened cotton trousers with metal rivets, while German business partner **LEVI STRAUSS** publicized the new "jeans". On 20 May 1873, the duo received the patent and this date is considered the *birthday of jeans*.

Style secrets

The tough new workwear was made from a fabric called **DENIM**, said to have originated in the port of Nîmes, France. A woven mix of *blue and white* cotton threads, it is the distinctive weave of the material that makes it so strong. The dark **indigo** dye was perfect for clothes that were not washed very often.

How it changed...

Jeans have become an enduring fashion fixture – they are the one item of clothing that never goes out of style.

the world

Jeans are named after sailors from Genoa, Italy, who wore tough blue trousers

Denim jeans

From humble roots to GLOBAL STYLE ICON, how denim jeans took over the world's wardrobes

Forever in blue jeans

The first jeans were so loose that they needed **braces** to stay up. By the mid-20th century, dressing down in denim proved a hit with the *younger generation* thanks to the cowboys of Western films and pop stars such as **ELVIS PRESLEY** wearing tighter, trendier versions. Today, jeans come in many different cuts and colours.

Selling soles

Sports shoes were up and running by the mid-19th century, after American *Charles Goodyear* invented vulcanized rubber. Billed as the flexible alternative to leather, the rubber-soled **SPORTS SHOE** was adopted by the US Rubber Company in 1892, which established the Keds business in 1917 to make and market the shoes.

Sports shoes

New shoes for athletes and sports enthusiasts FIND THEIR FEET in the mass market

In the USA, 350 million pairs are sold a year

High tops protect the ankle.

How it changed...
Rubber-soled shoes allowed sportspeople to go further and faster, and have become the first-choice footwear for millions.
the world

Groundbreaking design

Soon many companies were producing shoes that combined comfort and style. Lightweight **canvas uppers** allowed air to circulate, while laces were loosened or tightened as required. The shoes were nicknamed "**SNEAKERS**" because their vulcanized rubber soles let the wearer sneak about without being heard.

Thick rubber soles cushion the foot.

Laces fed through metal eyelets (holes).

Modern runarounds

In the 1930s, shoe companies began tailoring trainers to *sports*. Studs were screwed into football boots for better support, clips were added to cycling shoes to prevent slippage, and spikes on sprinting shoes improved grip. Today's **hi-tech trainers** include automatically adjusting cushioning systems that adapt to the individual wearer and specific surface to ensure peak performance.

Musical instruments

Innovative instruments have brought MUSIC to the ears of the masses

Musical instruments have existed since prehistoric times. As materials and designs have evolved, primitive versions have been fine-tuned, while new models strike a chord with musicians and audiences alike.

A Stradivarius violin sold in 2011 for a massive £9.8 million ⇨

This ornate, painted harpsichord was made in Antwerp in 1643.

Keyboard

For centuries, keyboards were used to sound organ pipes. But in the 15th century they began to be used to sound *strings*, and the **HARPSICHORD** was born. Pressing a key plucked a string, with each string playing a note. The **piano** arrived in the 18th century with its sophisticated keyboard of **WHITE AND BLACK** keys. Pianos use hammers to strike the strings, so the notes can be sounded loudly or quietly depending on how hard the key is pressed.

Violin

The smallest, *highest-pitched* member of the string family is the violin. Developed in the 16th century, the invention is usually attributed to Italian **ANDREA AMATI** who made an early version to entertain King Charles IX of France. The instrument was enhanced over the following two centuries into the **wooden wonder** recognizable today. This example was made by famous Italian violin-maker Antonio Stradivari in 1709.

Flute

Woodwind instruments consist of a hollow tube attached to a mouthpiece. When blown, **air inside vibrates** to produce sound. The flute is a popular example. Early flutes were simple and wooden, but developed into metal models with **COMPLEX KEYWORK**. German inventor *Theobald Boehm* hit the right note in the 19th century with his system of pads over holes, operated by keys or fingers.

Trumpet

This instrument has blown audiences away since ancient times. People in China signalled with trumpets from 1500 BCE, while Egyptian *King Tutankhamun*'s tomb contained trumpets similar to the ones shown on the right. Nowadays made from **BRASS**, the trumpet is famous for its strong sound. In the 1820s, German instrument-makers Stölzel and Blühmel created trumpets with **valves** to produce more notes.

Drum

While many **PERCUSSION** instruments require precise force for the perfect sound, the drum marches to its own beat. Drums have been discovered in ancient Mesopotamia (modern-day Iraq) dating back **5,000 years**. From tribal rituals and military conflicts to medieval dances and rock concerts, this instrument has always drummed up atmosphere. This drum was used by a **Confederate soldier** during the American Civil War (1861–1865).

Video games

The development of electronic games to play at home has brought FUN AND GAMES to players all over the world

Past play

Coin-operated **ARCADE GAMES** in public places were popular in the 1970s. Then, in 1975, Atari launched a home video version of the bat-and-ball arcade game **Pong**, and the games revolution was born. Companies released *new console formats* and games to the growing market. By 1980, **Pac-Man** made the leap to home video, becoming one of the **MOST POPULAR** games ever.

Game on

The 1990s saw computer giants including **Nintendo**, **SEGA**, and **Sony** competing for dominance in the video games console market. Their portable, handheld devices and improved graphics allowed **YOUNG ENTHUSIASTS** to play while on the move, with action and sport the main genres of game. Nintendo's *Game Boy* format was first choice for a generation of players, selling in excess of 118 million units.

How it changed... the world

Video games have caught the public imagination and become big business – the global gaming market was worth $66 billion in 2013.

Realistic special effects and surround sound are features of today's video games.

Ahead of the game

Instead of joysticks and keypads, **today's games** are played on home computers, advanced games consoles, mobile phones, or tablets. *Virtual reality* games give players the chance to inhabit incredible three-dimensional lands where they create their own characters, called **avatars**, and **INTERACT** with other players.

Vibrant, detailed graphics enhance the playing experience.

Music on the move

The personal stereo was the brainchild of **MASARU IBUKA**, chairman of Japanese electronics company Sony, who wanted to combine a **compact tape recorder** with *lightweight headphones*. The Walkman was launched in 1979. This handy, portable device saw users listening to their favourite **CASSETTES** while out and about. By 1982, more than 100 million had been sold.

Lightweight headphones and no external speaker gave a private listening experience.

A small screen showed which track on the CD was playing.

How it changed...
The Walkman allowed people to take their choice of tunes wherever they went. Today's MP3 owners are spoilt for choice with song selection.
the world

Personal stereo

These revolutionary portable devices have ensured pop fans can STAY TUNED to the music they love

Compact choice

As *compact discs* began to replace cassettes in the music market, **Sony** introduced the industry's first portable player for compact discs in 1982. The **DISCMAN** was a success among music lovers, but the device could carry only **one disc** at a time and had a tendency to skip.

Tiny tunes

German inventors **DIETER SEITZER** and **KARLHEINZ BRANDENBURG** came up with a way of compressing digital music, so that a music file takes up much less space. Their format is called MP3 and manufacturers used it to make small digital music players. The first MP3 player became available in 1998. These **groundbreaking gizmos** can store thousands of songs.

Cinema

Making pictures MOVE on the big screen

The history of the big screen features an all-star cast of inventors, stories of success, and a fun ending.

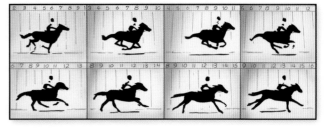

Picture pioneers

English doctor P M Roget found that seeing an object in **similar positions** over a rapid sequence, like this one of a horse running, resulted in the object *appearing to move*. In 1824, he called this "persistence of vision". Inventors wanted to create a better way to produce the **ILLUSION** of moving images from still ones.

By the way...
By inventing the Cinematograph, we became masters of the short film, with more than 1,000 clips to our names.

French premiere

The first to figure it out were the French brothers **Auguste and Louis Lumière**. They held the first public showing of projected moving images in a Parisian café basement in 1895. Their combined portable camera and projector, the *Cinematograph*, recorded "moving pictures" on a strip of celluloid film. The premiere was a hit with the paying audience and hailed the start of the **MOTION PICTURE** era.

Film firsts...

SILENT MOVIES *were replaced by "talkies" (films with dialogue and music), with* **THE JAZZ SINGER** *the first release in 1927.*

©A.M.P.A.S.®

The annual film awards ceremony called the Academy Awards, or **OSCARS**, *began in Hollywood, USA, in 1929.*

First film

The first films by the Lumière brothers caused a **SENSATION**. One depicted people leaving a factory, while another showed a **train arriving at a station** (above). Though today's blockbusters use new technology and special effects, films remain just a series of *separate images played in quick succession*.

The film passes through the projector, stopping for a moment on each frame.

The magic lantern provides a bright light that passes through the film.

How it changed the world

Cinema created the movie industry, which has enthralled audiences for decades and made stars of the actors appearing in its films. People around the world spend about £19.2 billion ($30 billion) on cinema tickets every year.

The lens focuses and directs the light onto a screen so the film can be seen.

Did you know?
In the 1930s, cinemas were decorated with chandeliers and carpets. They were so lavish that audiences called them "picture palaces".

In 1932 the Technicolor company released a camera that made colour film possible, with **THE WIZARD OF OZ** one of the first releases.

Now known as **BOLLYWOOD**, the Indian film industry boomed from the 1950s with hundreds of new releases every year.

Fireworks

Based on explosive gunpowder, show-stealing fireworks have a colourful past.

Celebrating with a BANG!

Chinese launch

GUNPOWDER was discovered accidentally when ancient Chinese alchemists looked for a magic potion to create **eternal life**. It was produced by mixing three powders – *saltpeter*, *sulphur*, and *charcoal*. When burned, the combination released so much gas that **EXPLOSIONS** resulted. Bamboo poles filled with gunpowder formed the first ever fireworks. They were used to mark **festivals** and **religious occasions**.

Today's fireworks use compressed air on release, so their displays are not obliterated by smoke.

It paved the way for...

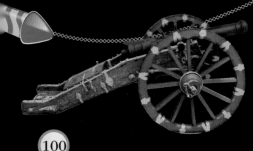

CANNONS *containing gunpowder and other explosives were an* **EFFECTIVE WEAPON** *when fired across battlefields during the Middle Ages.*

The Chinese used fireworks to create devices called **FLARES**. *These blazing lights could* **SIGNAL** *over long distances.*

Colours are determined by different combinations of chemicals.

Gunpowder plot

In the Middle Ages, rockets became **weapons**, catapulted into enemy bases to explode on impact and set camps alight. Famous English conspirator **GUY FAWKES** plotted a similarly dastardly deed with gunpowder. His failed attempt to *blow up* London's Houses of Parliament on 5 November 1605 is remembered every year with effigies of Fawkes **BURNED AT FIREWORK DISPLAYS**.

Spectrum of colour

The future's *glowing bright* for fireworks. Colour chemistry has developed a rainbow effect – magnesium and aluminium mix in **white** light, sodium salts shine **yellow**, copper salts produce **blue**, strontium nitrate or carbonate shows **red**, and barium nitrate creates **green**. Scientists are researching different **CHEMICAL COMBINATIONS** in order to make ever more impressive fireworks.

HOW IT WORKS

Once lit, the fuse allows you to retreat to a safe distance before the fuel propellant sends the firework into the sky. Once there, a part of the fuse called the delay controls when the chemical reaction in the rocket happens by slowing the ignition of the gunpowder. When the gunpowder is lit, it creates loud banging sounds and shoots the stars out of the firework.

Gunpowder

Stars

Delay

Propellant

Lit fuse

How it changed

Fireworks have delighted audiences for centuries, but the gunpowder at their core has also been used as a devastating weapon of war.

the world

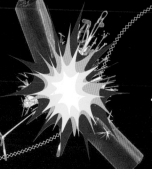

The strong, stable explosive called **DYNAMITE** is developed from gunpowder. Used in **CONSTRUCTION**, *it is also a harmful* **WEAPON**.

Key dates are celebrated with **FIREWORKS DISPLAYS**. *On New Years Eve, many countries set off fireworks at midnight to* **WELCOME THE COMING YEAR**.

Chocolate

For centuries chocolate was a bitter drink, but it became a famously favoured food when the ingredients were sweetened and solid chocolate was invented.

Nature's SWEETEST treat

Food of the gods

Chocolate has its roots in the cacao tree, *Theobroma cacao*. This Latin name means **"food of the gods"**, and the tree has long flourished in the hot climate of Central and South America. Inside each colourful fruit pod is sweet juice and **BITTER CACAO BEANS** – the essential ingredient of chocolate.

Ancient chocolatiers

Cacao beans were an integral part of ancient life in Mexico and Central America, with the **Inca, Aztec, and Maya peoples** the first true chocolatiers. They mixed cacao beans with spices to create a bitter drink called *chocolatl*, from which chocolate takes its name. Believing the beans had **MAGICAL PROPERTIES**, they used the drink in their sacred birth, marriage, and death rituals.

It paved the way for...

*Swiss chocolatier **DANIEL PETER** added condensed milk to the recipe in 1875 and invented **MILK CHOCOLATE** bars.*

*Fellow Swiss chocolatier **RODOLPHE LINDT** created the process of **CONCHING** in 1879, which produced smooth chocolate without the gritty texture it had previously.*

Chocolate houses

In the 16th century, European **CONQUISTADORS** arrived in the Americas and discovered the cacao beans. Realizing the commercial opportunity, Spanish conqueror Hernando Cortéz sweetened the chocolatl drink with cane sugar to cater to European tastes. In the 17th century, **fashionable chocolate houses** were popping up across Europe where high society could savour the new taste. *Only the wealthy* could afford this sweet treat.

Birth of the bar

In 1828, Dutch chemist Casparus Van Houten invented **powdered chocolate** or "Dutch cacao". Englishman Joseph Fry then added melted cacao butter to Dutch cacao in 1847, producing chocolate paste. **SOLID CHOCOLATE** was born! In 1868, English chocolate company Cadbury began making and marketing *bars of chocolate*. The tasty new treat quickly spread around the world.

How it changed the world

Chocolate is one of the world's favourite flavours, and one of the most lucrative: the modern chocolate industry is expected to be worth a mouthwatering £65 billion by 2016. Though doctors recommend chocolate in moderation, scientists are investigating the many chemicals in chocolate for any health benefits.

Known as "the Great American Chocolate Bar", the **HERSHEY BAR** *went on sale in 1900. It became one of the world's best-selling chocolate bars.*

The founding of the **NEW YORK COCOA EXCHANGE** *in 1925 recognized cacao as an important* **STOCK COMMODITY** *that could be bought and sold on the open market.*

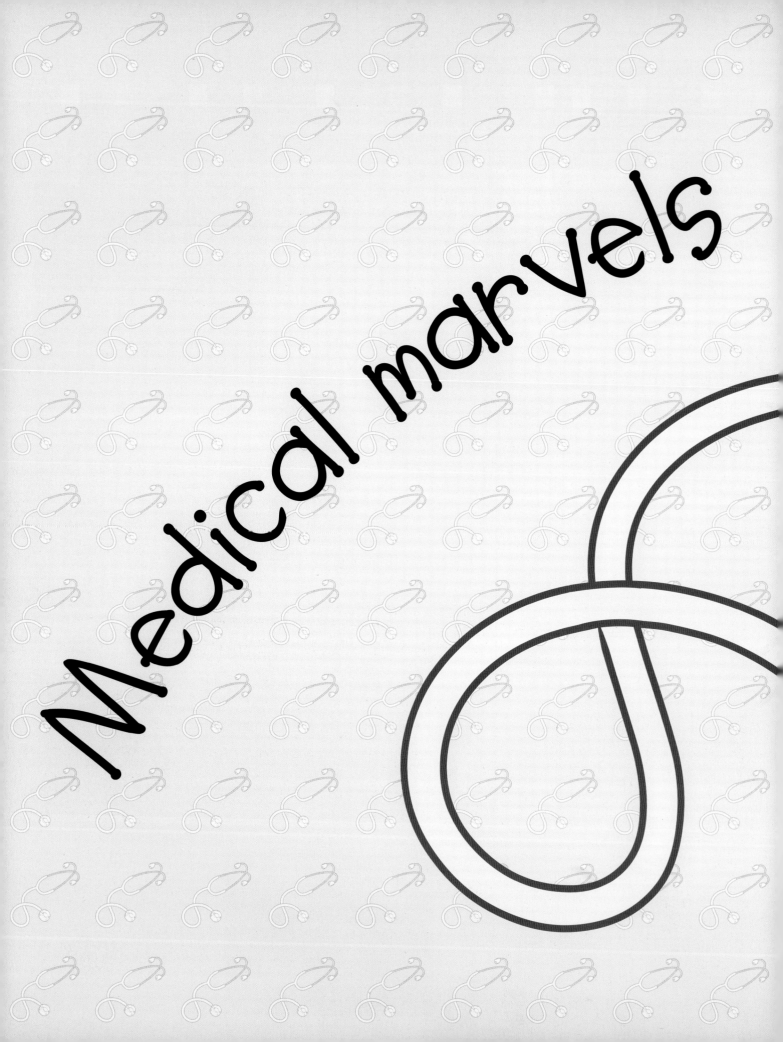

Medical marvels

The medical world was under the weather for centuries due to a basic lack of understanding. Now it is the picture of good health, thanks to our awareness of cleanliness and safety in treatments. Improvements in equipment have followed doctor's orders, making them a welcome addition to surgeries and hospitals. Forward-thinking inventions have gone for a check-up, been given the all-clear, and are now put to the best use – saving patients' lives.

Wide awake

Surgery in the past was **BRUTAL**. Patients were left wide awake or groggy with alcohol as cuts were made in their bodies. The *pain or shock* often resulted in death. Then, in 1846, American dentist **William Morton** discovered that he could use the chemical ether to make a person unconscious before surgery.

Rubber hose carries air and ether fumes from the jar to the mouthpiece to be breathed in.

Small pieces of sponge soaked in ether give off fumes.

Chloroform

Discovered in 1831, chloroform was first used as an anaesthetic by Scottish physician **James Young Simpson** in 1847. He used it to provide **PAIN RELIEF** for women, including Queen Victoria, during childbirth. However, chloroform had *dangerous side effects*. Some devices, like this Dubois machine (left) tried to make it safer by mixing it with air.

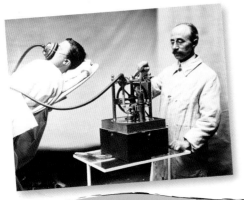

Anaesthetics

Putting patients to SLEEP was the first step towards modern surgical techniques

How it changed...

Before anaesthetics, surgery was quick, brutal, and often deadly. Now operations can be carried out easily and safely.

the world

Modern techniques

Today, anaesthetics can be **local** (numbing a body part such as a foot) or *general* (making a patient unconscious). Amylocaine was the first human-made local anaesthetic developed by French chemist **ERNEST FOURNEAU** in 1903. Some general anaesthetics are *administered using an injection* and work in less than 30 seconds. Others are given as a carefully-controlled dose to be breathed in.

Germ theory

People in the past *didn't understand* how infections occurred. Doctors operated in **dirty, germ-ridden conditions** and thought bad air was to blame. In the mid-19th century, French scientist **LOUIS PASTEUR** showed that some diseases and many infections were caused by bacteria and other microorganisms invading the body.

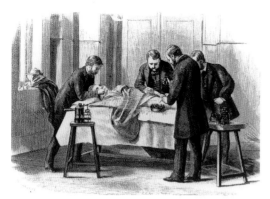

How it changed...
Antiseptics helped make surgery cleaner and far safer. Operations became more common and new types of surgery could be developed.
the world

Antiseptics

How microbe-killing substances CLEANED UP medicine's act so wounds could heal

Reservoir contains water mixed with carbolic acid.

Handle acts as a lever operating the small pump.

Pump nozzle sends out a fine mist of carbolic acid.

Lister method

British surgeon **JOSEPH LISTER** became convinced that *microbes in the air* were causing infections in wounds, which were usually left open. In the 1860s, Lister started to **clean wounds** and **soak dressings** in carbolic acid – the first antiseptic – which killed many infection-causing microbes. He also built a "**DONKEY ENGINE**" (left) to spray carbolic acid mist throughout his operating theatre. Infection and death rates after surgery *plummeted*.

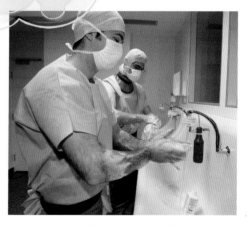

Keeping it clean

From the 1890s onwards, surgical instruments were boiled to sterilize them, *ridding them of all microbes* before use. Face masks were adopted and surgeons now **CLEAN THEIR HANDS** with antiseptic solutions before surgery. Rates of infection have been slashed from 50 per cent to less than 1 per cent.

107

Antibiotics

These wonder drugs are one of medicine's most important weapons in the fight against disease-causing bacteria. But the first antibiotic was discovered entirely by accident.

Stopping DISEASES in their tracks

Florey and Chain

Fleming had chanced upon the first antibiotic, but *isolating penicillin* in quantities large enough to treat people took more than a decade. A team in Oxford, England, led by Australian scientist **Howard Florey** used hospital bedpans and cow-milking equipment to produce enough penicillin to run **MEDICAL TRIALS** on humans in 1941. They proved successful in fighting a range of infections and diseases.

Ernst Chain proved penicillin's success in fighting bacteria in mammals through experiments with mice.

By the way...
I was a key member of Howard Florey's team. Along with Florey and Alexander Fleming I was awarded the 1945 Nobel Prize for Medicine.

Fleming's fluke

By the 19th century, scientists had worked out that many diseases are caused by **microscopic living things** called bacteria. In 1928, Scottish bacteriologist **ALEXANDER FLEMING** noticed that one of his petri dishes containing *Staphylococcus* bacteria had become contaminated with a blue mould, which seemed to have wiped out the bacteria. Fleming realized that the mould contained a bacteria-killing chemical, which he called **PENICILLIN**.

It paved the way for...

STREPTOMYCIN *was first made in 1943 by American scientist* **SELMAN WAKSMAN** *from bacteria found in soil. It was the first antibiotic remedy for tuberculosis.*

TETRACYCLINE *was first discovered in 1945 and then made in labs by US drug company Pfizer in the early 1950s. It became the* **MOST PRESCRIBED** *antibiotic in the USA.*

TETRACYCLINE 30 mcg

Mass production

Florey's **successful trials** led US drug companies to start producing the drug in large quantities. The first stocks of penicillin were sent to help soldiers wounded in **WORLD WAR II**, and dramatically reduced the number of deaths from infected wounds. After the war, the new drug was in demand to *combat diseases* such as pneumonia, scarlet fever, gangrene, and diphtheria.

Howard Florey worked with drugs companies in the USA to produce large quantities of penicillin.

Vials of penicillin were packed along with other battlefield medicines to treat wounded soldiers during World War II.

Amazing antivirals

Viruses are different from bacteria. They invade healthy cells and force them to copy the virus so that it spreads. **GERTRUDE B ELION** was an American chemist who developed the first widely available antiviral drug, *acyclovir*, in the 1970s. It was used to treat the herpes virus, which causes coldsores. She later **came out of retirement** to help create AZT, the first anti-HIV drug.

How it changed the world

The discovery of penicillin saved millions of lives, but it also led to a revolution in the development of new drugs, with many more antibiotics following in its wake. Along with antivirals, these drugs have provided safe treatments for countless conditions.

ELIZABETH LEE HAZEN *and* RACHEL FULLER BROWN *patented the antibiotic* NYSTATIN *in 1957. It is used to fight fungal infections.*

Microscope

The device that uses light passing through a lens to FOCUS ON a miniscule world of wonders

Focusing screw

Handle

Lens

Optical microscopes

Like all early microscopes, this 1670 model used by English scientist Robert Hooke is an example of an optical microscope. It features a **SERIES OF LENSES** in a barrel. The lens closest to the object being studied *focuses light to form a magnified image*, which can then be magnified further by an ocular lens (eyepiece). Still widely used by scientists, **modern optical microscopes** can reach magnification of up to 1,000 times.

Holder for the specimen (the object focused on by the microscope).

Hooke was able to see and illustrate fleas and other tiny things for the first time.

In focus

Father and son lens-makers, **HANS AND ZACHARIAS JANSSEN** experimented with *lenses in tubes* in the 1590s to make the first microscopes. They were able to **magnify their view** of small things by around ten times. Less than a century later, fellow Dutchman *Anton Van Leeuwenhoek* built microscopes (above) with 270x magnification.

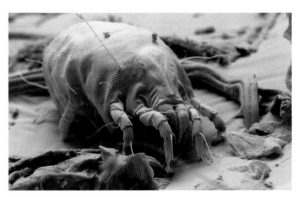

Electron microscopes

German physicist **ERNST RUSKA** developed microscopes in the 1930s that beamed *a stream of electrons* rather than light through a specimen. These can achieve far greater magnification – up to an amazing **500,000 times**. Incredibly small objects such as this dust mite can be seen in astonishing detail.

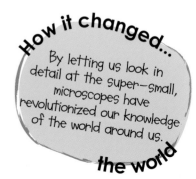

How it changed...
By letting us look in detail at the super-small, microscopes have revolutionized our knowledge of the world around us. **the world**

First laser

The first working laser was produced in 1960. A ruby crystal rod (above) was placed inside a photographer's flash lamp. When the atoms in the rod were excited by light from the flash, they generated energy as an intense pulse of red light. The ruby laser was a research tool, without a practical use.

How it changed... the world

Aside from their use in industry and surgery, lasers are used in all sorts of objects, from CD players to laser printers.

Laser surgery

Lasers also perform *valuable medical work*. They can weld a detached retina back into place and correct myopia (short-sightedness). They can also seal blood vessels and act as a **highly accurate scalpel**, destroying harmful or diseased cells with precision.

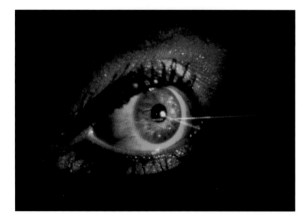

Cutting-edge technology

Today, many different kinds of lasers are produced to perform *dozens of different tasks* in industry. **INDUSTRIAL LASERS** wielded by robots (above) can be focused tightly on a single spot to drill holes or **cut through thick metal** and other tough materials accurately. Some lasers are used to weld metals together or to etch electronic circuits.

Laser

The instrument that focuses BEAMS OF LIGHT to perform amazing tasks in medicine and industry

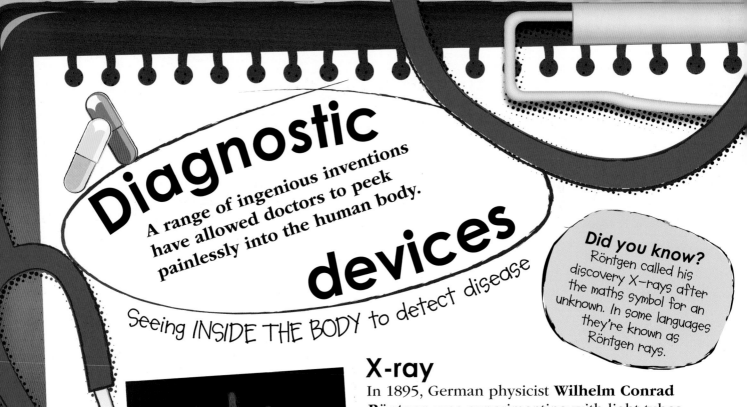

Diagnostic devices

A range of ingenious inventions have allowed doctors to peek painlessly into the human body.

Seeing INSIDE THE BODY to detect disease

Did you know?
Röntgen called his discovery X-rays after the maths symbol for an unknown. In some languages they're known as Röntgen rays.

X-ray

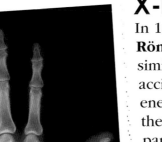

In 1895, German physicist **Wilhelm Conrad Röntgen** was experimenting with light tubes similar to fluorescent lamps when, by accident, he discovered mysterious waves of energy he called **X-RAYS**. Röntgen found that they passed through flesh and other soft parts of the body but *not through metal or bones*. When a special film is placed behind the body, it can capture an X-ray image. X-rays are now used to help **find broken bones** and pinpoint foreign objects, such as bullets, inside the body.

Stethoscope

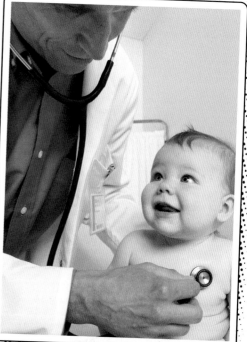

Stethoscopes let doctors check for problems by listening to a patient's *heartbeat and breathing* as well as the sound of blood rushing round blood vessels. French doctor **RENÉ LAENNEC** invented the first stethoscope, a simple wooden tube, in **1816**. Modern stethoscopes have a diaphragm that picks up sounds and *makes them louder* before they travel to the doctor's ears.

Stethoscope eartips go in the doctor's ears to hear your breathing and heartbeat.

Ultrasound

Sounds higher than those you can hear are called **ULTRASOUND**. An ultrasound scanner sends out these sounds into a patient's body. Different types of tissue such as *bone or muscle* produce a different echo. The machine listens to the different echoes and builds up a picture called an **echogram** or **sonogram**. The first echogram was produced in 1958. Ultrasound is especially used to check on *babies in the womb*.

Stethoscope diaphragm is placed on the skin closest to the part of the body inside that the doctor wants to listen to.

Fibre-optic endoscope

An endoscope is a narrow, flexible tube that travels inside part of your body so that doctors can take a good look. Researchers at the **UNIVERSITY OF ALABAMA** invented the first fibre-optic endoscope in **1957**. These contain bundles of thousands of *thin glass fibres*, which carry images from inside your body to be displayed on a screen.

Oral thermometers are placed under the tongue to measure temperature. A healthy human body's temperature is about 36.8°C (98.2°F).

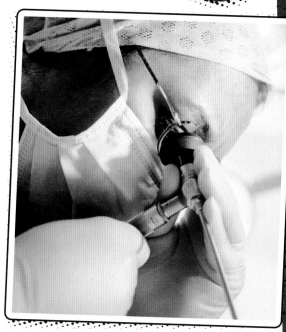

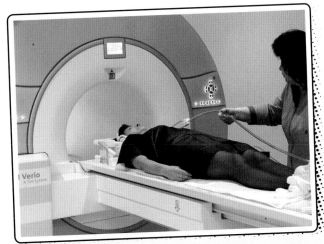

MRI scan

When placed in a magnetic field and bombarded with radio waves, atoms in your body **answer back**. The tiny signals they give off can be gathered and turned into a detailed picture of what's going on inside the body using a *Magnetic Resonance Imager* (MRI). The first MRI to perform a full scan of the body was invented by American professor **RAYMOND V DAMADIAN** in 1977.

Barking up the right tree

SALICYLIC ACID is a substance that helps **reduce pain** in the body's nerve endings. This means it's good at relieving such **common complaints** as headaches, swellings, and muscle aches. Some plants, such as meadowsweet and the bark of the willow tree, **are rich in salicylic acid**. Willow bark was used as a remedy for fever in ancient Greece, more than two thousand years ago.

Willow bark chips were used as a herbal remedy.

How it changed...

Aspirin is now the most widely used drug for pain relief in the world. Around 100 billion tablets are taken every year.

the world

Aspirin was first sold as a powder in tins.

Aspirin

The handy HUMBLE PILL that gives fevers the elbow and headaches the heave-ho

Mixing it up

Salicylic acid **TASTED AWFUL** and could cause vomiting and stomach upsets, so various chemists in the 19th century worked to find ways to **remove its bad side effects**. In 1897, chemists in Germany produced **acetylsalicylic acid (ASA)**, which caused less upset but was still an effective pain reliever. German chemicals company, Friedrich Bayer & Co., began selling ASA in 1899 under the brand name **ASPIRIN**.

Plastic bottle often comes with a child-proof lid.

Wonder drug

In 1900, aspirin was first sold as tablets that **dissolve in water**, the first medicine to be sold in this form. It was taken to ease **HEADACHES AND FEVERS**, and by people who suffer from rheumatism to reduce pain in their joints. More recent research suggests that aspirin can help **prevent blood clotting** and may even have a role in fighting Alzheimer's disease and certain cancers.

Tablets contain a set dose of aspirin mixed with corn starch and water.

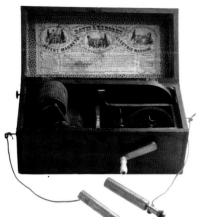

Shocking story

Scientists in the 19th and early 20th centuries learned that an **electric shock** could restart a heart or correct it when it started beating abnormally. The first defibrillators passed an electric current through *wires touching the heart* and could be used only in hospitals during an **OPERATION**.

Paddles are placed on the patient's body.

Closed chest

Closed chest defibrillators can correct heart rhythms or restart a heart *without the body being opened up*. The first units were huge, expensive, and needed mains electricity. In 1965, Northern Irish doctor **FRANK PANTRIDGE** built a defibrillator powered by car batteries and developed **smaller, portable models** to be carried in ambulances.

An electric current flows between the two paddles and through the heart.

Instructions show the first aider how to use the equipment.

How it changed...
Every minute a heart stops decreases the chances of survival. Defibrillators provide on-the-spot help, saving thousands of lives.
the world

Defibrillator

The SHOCKING invention that saves lives by restarting hearts

Modern design

Modern defibrillators are **lightweight** and found in many places, from swimming pools to schools, not just medical centres. Some give *spoken instructions* so that any adult can use them in an emergency.

Vaccination

Vaccination exposes a person to a mild form of a disease, so that his or her body learns to fight the disease in the future.

This pin device was used in 18th–century Europe to move infected tissue from one person to another.

Variolation

In the 10th century, the Chinese began a simple form of vaccination called **VARIOLATION**. They exposed healthy people to the disease smallpox, in the hope they would catch a milder version and, after recovery, *become immune*. A piece of a scab would be placed under the skin, or ground up and blown up a patient's nose. The practice spread to Europe, but the method was unreliable and could lead to the **spread of other diseases**.

Dairy cows carried the cowpox virus on their udders.

Milkmaids often caught cowpox, a disease caused by a virus related to but much milder than the deadly smallpox.

It paved the way for...

*In 1853, French doctor **Charles Pravaz** invented the practical metal **HYPODERMIC SYRINGE**. Used to administer vaccines, it has a hollow needle to pierce the skin.*

ROBERT KOCH *discovered the bacteria that cause **ANTHRAX** (1876), **TUBERCULOSIS** (1882), and **CHOLERA** (1883), allowing vaccines to be developed.*

Risky research

In the 18th century, smallpox was a **MAJOR KILLER**: around 400,000 people died of the disease every year in Europe alone. In 1796, English doctor **Edward Jenner** infected an eight-year-old boy with a small amount of cowpox pus. Cowpox was similar to smallpox but much less dangerous. *Success!* The boy proved immune to smallpox.

Edward Jenner realized that milkmaids who had caught cowpox were subsequently immune to smallpox.

By the way...
I sometimes vaccinated as many as 200 people a day. I also came up with the word, vaccine from "vacca", the Latin word for cow.

Vaccination station

A century later, French chemist **Louis Pasteur** made the next major breakthrough. In 1885, a young boy suffering from rabies arrived at his lab *close to death*. Pasteur had been experimenting with how a weakened form of rabies could be turned into a vaccine and gave the boy a **SERIES OF INJECTIONS**. The boy regained full health, Pasteur went on to vaccinate thousands of people, and today many vaccines are *still made using his methods*.

How it changed the world

Many were horrified at Jenner's work but vaccination caught on. In 1979, the World Health Organization declared that smallpox had finally been wiped out. Pasteur's work led to research into other vaccines, and today we are protected against many once-common killers.

Swiss-born doctor **ALEXANDRE YERSIN** *created a vaccine against* DIPHTHERIA *and in 1894 discovered the Yersinia pestis bacteria that caused* **BUBONIC PLAGUE**.

HIV *is a devastating virus that breaks down the human body's immune system.* **MASSIVE RESEARCH** *is ongoing to discover a vaccine against HIV.*

Bionic body bits

Poorly performing parts can be replaced by these medical miracles.

Lending us a HAND – amongst other body bits

The ball of the prosthetic hip joint fits into the socket in the pelvis.

 Hip joints can be replaced to relieve arthritis

The spiked end is fitted into a hole drilled in the femur (upper leg bone).

Artificial limbs

The first known **prosthesis** (artificial body part) was a **WOODEN TOE** found on a 2,700-year-old Egyptian mummy. Since that time, *artificial hands, feet, arms, and legs* have all been made. Early ones were forged from metal or carved from wood. Some wooden hands (above) had hinged finger joints and could be locked in a gripping position to **hold objects**.

Hearing aid

Early hearing aids were big funnels called **EAR TRUMPETS** that channelled sound waves from the air into the ear. Some were made from silver and *decorated ornately* whilst others were hidden in walking sticks to save users' embarrassment. Modern hearing aids use a microphone to pick up sounds and an **electronic amplifier** to make them louder, before they are replayed close to or inside the ear.

Contact lenses

Early contact lenses were made of **HARD GLASS** and were often very uncomfortable to wear. Czech chemist **Otto Wichterle** experimented at home with hydrogels (types of polymer material that hold water). In 1961, he built a machine on his kitchen table out of *parts from a child's construction kit* and a record player motor. It span out tiny discs of the material, which formed the first comfortable soft contact lenses.

Dentures

Many kinds of **FALSE TEETH**, also known as dentures, have been in use over centuries. The Etruscans in northern Italy made dentures from human and animal teeth from about 700 BCE. George Washington, the first president of the USA, wore dentures *carved out of hippopotamus ivory* and held in place by springs made of gold wire. Modern dentures are made from **plastics**, and are coloured and shaped to look like the real thing.

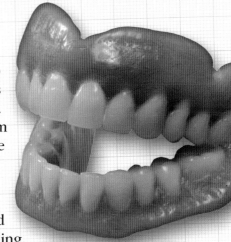

Pacemaker

Some people's hearts don't beat at a healthy rate or rhythm. Pacemakers help by sending out small **ELECTRICAL PULSES** to stimulate the heart muscles. One of the first, built by Canadian **John Hopps** in 1950, was the size of a toaster and needed to be plugged into a wall socket. Nine years later came a successful *implantable* pacemaker placed completely inside the body. Some patients lived for 30 years with this model, developed by Americans, **Wilson Greatbatch** and **William Chardack**.

Glass eyeballs don't help people see but they look realistic

Micro machines

Minimum size with MAXIMUM potential

A nanometre is one-billionth of a metre or about the width of ten atoms. A single human hair is about 80,000 nanometres wide. Recent scientific advances mean that machines and materials are starting to be constructed on this phenomenally small scale.

Thinking small

The concepts behind *nanotechnology* were first discussed in 1959 by US physicist **RICHARD FEYNMAN** in his talk, "There's Plenty of Room at the Bottom". He urged scientists to **think small** and build technology out of mere atoms.

Scientists started at the **MICROSCALE**, measured in thousandths of a millimetre, building motors, gears, electronic circuits, and even *sunglasses for houseflies*! Microprocessor chips found in smartphones and PCs feature millions of switches and circuits etched onto a circuit board **smaller than a fingernail**.

It paved the way for...

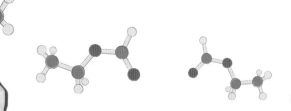

Many clothing manufacturers already sell **STAIN-RESISTANT** *clothes that contain tiny particles called* **NANO-WHISKERS**, *which stop stains from sticking to the fabric.*

There are 600 **NANOFOODS** *on the market today, including a variety of canola oil that can* **BLOCK CHOLESTEROL** *from entering the bloodstream.*

Marvellous microscope

In 1981, the **Scanning Tunnelling Microscope** (STM) was invented by German scientists **GERD BINNIG** and **HEINRICH ROHRER**. It uses a needle tip just a few atoms wide to scan an object, tracing out the surface atoms and spaces between them to form an image. STMs work at **incredible resolutions**, capable of *showing us individual atoms*. They also allow scientists to work at the nano scale directly, moving and manipulating individual atoms for the first time.

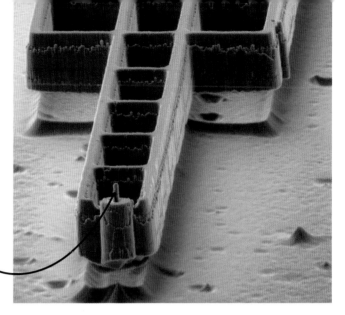

This highly magnified view shows an STM's needle.

Nanobot injects treatment directly into cell.

Life-saving nanobots

Now that scientists are able to work on the nanoscale, *the possibilities are endless*. One key application in the future could be **MEDICAL NANOBOTS** – tiny robots injected into the body. Some might scrub blood vessels clean of fats whilst others could **repair damage** from the inside, or (left) track, capture, and deal with harmful bacteria or diseased cells. *Swarms of nanobots* might monitor you from the inside to give your body a continual check up.

Diseased cell

Did you know?
These micro-cogs, shown here next to a fly's leg, were made using techniques that can work to thousandths of a millimetre.

How it changed the world

The answer is…we don't know yet, as all things nano are only just starting. But they could revolutionise the way we live in the future.

NANOPARTICLES *of metal oxides are used in some* **SUNSCREENS**. *They offer protection from the Sun but don't leave white marks on the skin.*

GRAPHENE *is a remarkable material with many potential applications. It is made of* **CARBON ATOMS** *joined in hexagons that form a surface a single atom thick.*

121

Total turkeys

For every high-flying GENIUS invention, there are countless other ones that never make it OFF THE GROUND.

1801 Captain Dick's Puffer

British inventor **RICHARD TREVITHICK** lost his train of thought when he left the engine of *his first passenger steam carriage* running while he stopped off for a swift beverage. All the water in the engine boiled off and poor old Captain Dick's Puffer **exploded**. But Trevithick got back on track two years later with his celebrated creation, the steam locomotive.

1862 Hunley's submarine

American engineer Horace Hunley had that sinking feeling when his submarine for the **American Civil War** came to a disastrous end. The underwater weapon had been developed from an old boiler and was **ARMED WITH A TORPEDO**. Hunley's design managed to sink an enemy ship, but the sub itself exploded at the same time, and joined its target *on the sea bed*.

1874 De Groof parachute

With his eyes firmly on the skies, Belgian Vincent De Groof longed to fly like a bird. His vision came to life with a **WINGED PARACHUTE** that he *attached to a balloon* to soar over London. When the wings fell apart mid-flight, the birdbrain's feathers were **well and truly ruffled**. In a flap, he hit the ground, ending his dream and his life.

1880s Suitcase lifejacket

A German named Krankel built a case for a lifejacket – literally. His suitcase had two removable panels just *in case of an emergency*. Water-wearers took out the panels, blocked the hole with a rubber ring, and wriggled into the case. But **carrying excess baggage** didn't float everyone's boat and the invention quickly moved **FROM SUITCASE TO NUTCASE**.

1894 Maxim's flying machine

American-born innovator **HIRAM MAXIM** fired his way to success with the machine gun in 1884, but he crashed with his attempt at a **flying machine**. Despite five sets of wings spanning 38 m (125 ft), two steam engines, and a pair of propellers, the machine took off from rails and flew briefly before coming back down to Earth with *a very big bump*!

The mechanism worked best with dome-shaped bowler hats

1896 Self-raising hat

Back in Victorian times, it was all the rage for gentlemen to *tip their hats* when passing ladies on the street. Hats off, then, to American **JAMES BOYLE**, who made mechanics do the hard work with his self-tipping hat. When the wearer **gave the nod**, a clockwork device inside doffed the hat to the passing lady. Sadly for Boyle, the hat simply failed to raise the interest of customers, and it was hung up for good soon after.

1896 Power shower

A lean machine for **KEEPING CLEAN** was the brainchild of one particularly keen cyclist. It was basically a bicycle (without wheels) that used **pedal power** to pump water in the shower. The more pedalling, the better the power shower. Great for gym bunnies, but *not so easy for couch potatoes*. "Get on your bike!" was the general response to this fleeting fad.

Hen-pecking is common among cheeky chickens

1903 Chicken glasses

American Andrew Jackson developed *protective glasses* for his feathered friends to wear to stop them from hurting each other's eyes. Jackson assumed his **sight-saving invention** would provide a good nest egg, but it's a mistake to count your chickens before they are hatched. Though some glasses were sold in the USA at the turn of the century, they are now **nowhere to be seen**.

1922 Baby cage

For nannies left holding the baby in high-rise buildings, one last resort was **an outdoor cage**, into which you could put a baby. American inventor **EMMA READ**'s intentions were good: the plan was to give babies *fresh air and room to play*. In reality, though, there was much rattling of cages and baby blues all round.

1960 Smell-o-Vision

American movie maestro Mike Todd Jr believed he was on to the **sweet smell of success** with Smell-o-Vision. This new technology released odours during the showing of films to enhance the experience. *Scent of Mystery* was the only film to use Smell-o-Vision, and it was an absolute stinker. Audiences turned their noses up at the gimmick and Todd had to wake up and smell the coffee.

1962 Robot Readamatic

This robotic reading device was designed to speed up bookworms. At the **turn of a dial**, one line of text was displayed at a time. Though meant to develop the reader's pace, the design was **FATALLY FLAWED**, as the machine's loud whirring sound and distracting mechanical arm had users throwing the book at the invention.

1976 Rolling ball

Italian **ALESSANDRO DANDINI** came up with a bizarre new vessel for transporting cargo across the sea. He devised a plan to have *a big motorized ball* with two cabins attached on either side of it. Cargo could be stored inside the sphere or the cabins. However, the tipping point came when one cabin was detached, causing the whole lot to **flip on its side**. As a result, the marine machine didn't do the rounds for long.

1980s Nimslo 3–D camera

The combined efforts of American photography enthusiasts Jerry Nims and Allen Lo produced the Nimslo 3–D camera. The **snap-happy device** used four lenses, each taking one frame at a slightly different angle to make one 3–D image. Unfortunately the creators hadn't focused on the bigger picture. At **TEN TIMES THE PRICE** of a normal camera, consumers said no to Nimslo.

1982 APT

The Advanced Passenger Train was invented to tilt as it travelled round corners, but the idea **came off the rails** from the get-go. All the tipping and dipping at high-speed had passengers reaching for sick bags, frozen brakes posed a problem in cold spells, and some parts of the design got stuck at a slant! The tilting train was **GOING NOWHERE**.

2007 Phone Fingers

When Austrian **PHILIPP ZUMTOBEL** pointed a finger at the problem of smudges and marks on smart phones, his solution took the form of an accessory called Phone Fingers. These tight-fitting **rubber finger covers** are rolled onto the user's digits to keep keypads clean. However, the public gave the idea a *thumbs down* – most phone users fixed the original problem by simply washing their hands.

Phone Fingers were too difficult to get on and off the hands

Fantastic future

Nobody really knows what the great inventions of the FUTURE might be, but here's some that just might make the grade.

The silent plane's unique shape is the secret to its success

Space tourism

Thousands of space cadets have put their names down to **BOLDLY GO** where no one else has gone, with one-way trips to *Mars* scheduled for a decade's time. The intention is to establish a colony on the red planet – the **first human settlement** outside of Earth.

Human clones

It all began in 1997 when Dolly the sheep became the first *animal clone* (identical replica of an existing organism). Pigs, cows, dogs, and mice have since joined the clone zone, and now there's talk of **cloning people**. However, many governments have **BANNED** this controversial concept, preferring not to meddle with nature.

Hoverbike

Hi-tech hoverbikes could soon help commuters *rise above* the morning rat race. Powered by light **JET ENGINES**, this invention could float way above the traffic, taking the driver direct to his or her destination. As the world's roads become *increasingly jammed*, hoverbike users could **fly free as birds**.

Riding a hoverbike would make you stand out from the crowd

Sonic washer

Future washing machines may use **ultrasound and static electricity**, rather than soap and water. Popping ultrasound waves into your dirty laundry would **FREE THE FILTH**, while electrostatic attractors zap it away, trapping grime in a *murky mess* at the bottom.

Silent planes

Noisy air traffic can be a real bugbear for people living under flight paths. In future, those on the ground may enjoy **the sound of silence**, thanks to the work of Cambridge University in England, and the Massachusetts Institute of Technology in the USA. These educational forces are off to a **FLYING START** with a new aircraft so quiet that no one outside of an airport can hear it. As well as bringing peace and harmony, this is an *eco-friendly option*, burning far less fuel than today's aircraft.

Toothphone

Here's a hands-free invention to really sink your teeth into. Inventors are researching a toothphone to *direct-dial your gnashers*. With a mini microchip placed in one of your teeth, incoming calls would be heard by sending vibrations **along the jaw** straight into your ear. No more choosing handsets and phone covers! Just brush up on your dental hygiene to ensure your toothphone remains **ON CALL**.

Robot sports coaches

When you're *going for gold* at your favourite sport, you don't want a slow coach. To be the best, try hands-on training from **fully computerized sports coaches**. At 7 ft (2.1 m) tall, Robo-coach is ten times stronger than the average person. It can play any sport for **36 HOURS NON-STOP** before the batteries run out. Video cameras record performances and can be played back in 3-D on the robot's chest. If a session with Robo-coach leaves you exhausted, it will even give you *a relaxing massage*.

Video tattoos

Picture this – *an electronic display* printed on a fine plastic membrane and placed over your skin. This makes your body a **BLANK CANVAS**, able to showcase computer displays and change them to suit your mood. The electronic version moves and stretches without breaking, and if you ever regret that tattoo of your dead tortoise, **it's not permanent**!

Exoskeleton clothing

If your childhood wish was to be a superhero with special powers, an **EXOSKELETON** could make your dream come true. This body armour makes the wearer *as brawny as Batman*. The super-strength clothing is made from polymer gel muscles, which are five times stronger than natural fibres. These costly costumes will come down in price in future, making them **ideal protection** for the military and police services.

Air-conditioned suits

Keeping cool while suited and booted is a problem for business people in **HOT CLIMATES**. However, a new wardrobe winner is coming on the fashion scene. A suit jacket, secretly home to **two tiny fans** that suck in air to evaporate perspiration, will help keep business brains cool *even when the temperature rises*. The manufacturers claim that this is a small-scale, low-cost, and environmentally-friendly alternative to air-conditioning units.

Artificial meat

The invention of **LAB-GROWN MEAT** could one day take animals *off the menu*. Cells can now be taken from live animals and put in an environment where they are cultivated separately. In August 2013, a Dutch design team served the first **ARTIFICIAL BEEFBURGER** at a London launch. If customers get a taste for this cultured cuisine, fake meat could go the whole hog and turn into a **supermarket staple**. Right now, though, this protein is too pricey to be mainstream fodder.

The first lab-grown burger cost a whopping £200,000 to produce

High-altitude wind power

When it comes to harnessing the world's **natural energy resources**, the answer is blowing in the wind. Traditionally wind power is generated from *turbines on Earth*, but high above Earth's surface wind speeds are much faster, peaking in the jet streams of 8 km (5 miles) and above. Environmental agencies are blown away by the idea of **AIRBORNE TURBINES** suspended high up in the air, but tethered to the ground. With costly maintenance and aviation interference to consider, inventors are still shooting the breeze on this gusty idea.

Invisibility cloak

Ever wished you could be invisible, just like Harry Potter? In 2012, researchers from the USA's Duke University **made a small 3-D object invisible** using a flexible fabric called **META-FLEX**. Although the object disappeared as if by magic, it was really a *trick of the light*. The illusion worked because the fabric bent light away from the eyes and sent it around the object instead, making it seem as though nothing was there. The next stroke of wizardry is to **make people invisible** and inventors claim to have this within their sights.

Brain implants

When you're lacking in grey matter, imagine plugging in an *intellectual implant* to boost your brain in an instant. This mastermind module has already worked with primates, when implants were attached to the **PREFRONTAL CORTEX** (the area for thought, memory, and attention) of their brains. The decision-making skills of Rhesus monkeys improved by 10 per cent. Researching eggheads hope to adapt the implant for humans, taking the wearer **from bird-brain to brainbox** in one smooth move.

Glossary

Agricultural Revolution
The name given to the series of advancements in agriculture in Britain between 1600 and 1850.

Alchemy
The ancient study of matter, which aimed to discover the secret of everlasting life.

Astrolabe
A device used by sailors to measure the height of the sun in order to help them work out their ship's latitude.

Atom
The smallest part of an element that has the characteristics of that element.

Bollywood
The largest part of the Indian film industry, based in Bombay.

Conduction
The process by which heat or electricity passes through a substance.

Conquistador
One of the Spanish conquerors of the Native American civilizations.

Defibrillator
A machine that is used to correct or restart the beat of the human heart.

Electron
A subatomic particle with a negative charge that orbits an atom's nucleus.

Filament
The part of a light bulb that glows when an electric current is passed through it.

Gravity
The force that attracts all objects together. On Earth, it is responsible for making objects fall downwards and for giving things weight.

Industrial Revolution
The name given to the industrial expansion of Britain from about 1700.

Insulation
Reducing the flow of heat, to keep things cool or hot. Electrical insulation prevents electric current flowing.

Internal combustion engine
An engine in which fuel is burned (combusted) to create movement.

Internet
The interconnected network of computers that spans the globe.

Latitude
A measurement of how north or south of the equator a location is. Latitude lines on a map run from east to west.

Longitude
A measurement of how east or west of the Prime Meridian an object is. The Prime Meridian is an imaginary line that runs from the North Pole, via Greenwich, England, to the South Pole. Longitude lines run from north to south.

Microbe
A living thing that can be seen only through a microscope. Bacteria are the most common types of microbe.

Microprocessor
The complicated circuits at the heart of a computer that carry out instructions and calculations, and communicate with other parts of the computer.

Middle Ages
The period in European history between the fall of the Roman Empire in the 5th century and the Renaissance in the 1400s.

Molecule
The smallest amount of a compound, consisting of two or more atoms bonded together.

Morse code
A special kind of code that uses dots and dashes to represent letters, useful for long-distance communication.

Neutron
A subatomic particle with no electric charge found in an atom's nucleus.

Nuclear fission
A process in which a nucleus is split by firing neutrons at it to release energy.

Ozone layer
A layer in Earth's atmosphere with a high concentration of ozone, which absorbs harmful radiation from the Sun.

Patent
A government document that grants sole rights to a person to make, use, and/or sell an invention.

Piston
A round metal part that fits tightly inside a cylinder and moves back and forwards.

Proton
A subatomic particle with a positive charge found in an atom's nucleus.

Radio wave
A type of energy that is invisible, travels in waves, and can be used to send information, especially sound.

Sextant
A tool that measures the angle between the horizon and objects in the sky, useful for working out latitude.

Transistor
A tiny electronic component that is used to switch or amplify electric signals.

World Wide Web
Documents on the Internet that are linked together and navigated by a web browser.

USSR
The Union of Soviet Socialist Republics, also known as the Soviet Union, which existed from 1922 to 1991 and was succeeded by the Russian Federation.

Index

Acknowledgements

DK WOULD LIKE TO THANK:
Jackie Brind for the index, Carron Brown for proofreading, and
Julian Baker (www.jbillustrations.co.uk) for commissioned illustrations.

**THE PUBLISHER WOULD LIKE TO THANK THE
FOLLOWING FOR THEIR KIND PERMISSION TO
REPRODUCE THEIR PHOTOGRAPHS:**
Key: a–above; b–below/bottom; c–centre; f–far; l–left; r–right; t–top

1 Dorling Kindersley: The National Cycle Collection (bl). **8
Corbis:** (bc, br). **9 Dorling Kindersley:** Banbury Museum
(bl); The Science Museum, London (tl). **Fotolia:**
bevangoldswain (tl/Face); James Steidl (cl); Gennady
Poddubny (br); daseaford (crb). **10 The Bridgeman Art
Library:** De Agostini Picture Library / G. Dagli Orti (crb);
Museu Nacional de Arte Antigua, Lisbon, Portuga (c/Henry
the Navigator). **Corbis:** Bettmann (bl). **Dorling Kindersley:**
National Maritime Museum, London (c). **11 Corbis:**
Wolfgang Deuter (bl); The Mariners' Museum (c). **Mary
Evans Picture Library:** (tl). **12 Dreamstime.com:**
Chinaview (br). **13 Dorling Kindersley:** National Maritime
Museum, London (tr); National Maritime Museum, London
(clb). **Getty Images:** MyLoupe / Universal Images Group
(br). **14 Dorling Kindersley:** The Science Museum, London
(c). **Getty Images:** Science & Society Picture Library (br).
15 Corbis: Bettmann (cr). **Getty Images:** Science & Society
Picture Library (c). **16-17 Dorling Kindersley:** The
Science Museum, London (tc). **16 Corbis:** Leonard de
Selva (bc); Tarker (bl). **Dorling Kindersley:** The Science
Museum, London (cl). **Science Photo Library:** Sheila Terry
(cb); Usa Library Of Congress (tr). **17 Fotolia:** danr13 (bc).
18 Corbis: Brooks Kraft / Sygma (clb). **Dorling Kindersley:**
The National Motorcycle Museum (c). **Fotolia:** Tomasz
Trojanowski (bc). **Getty Images:** Science & Society Picture
Library (ca). **18-19 Dorling Kindersley:** The National Cycle
Collection (c). **19 Fotolia:** inigocia (cr). **20 Corbis:**
Bettmann (cr). **Dorling Kindersley:** Donks Models -
modelmaker (bl). **Getty Images:** Universal Images Group
(cl). **Wikipedia:** Konrad Kyeser: "Bellifortis" (Clm 30150)
(bc). **21 Corbis:** Lake County Museum (cr); PoodlesRock /
PoodlesRock (tc). **Fotolia:** victorhabbick (bc). **22 Alamy
Images:** Comstock Production Department / Comstock
Images (br). **Corbis:** Hulton-Deutsch Collection (tr).
Dorling Kindersley: The National Motor Museum, Beaulieu
(tl). **22-23 Getty Images:** Science & Society Picture
Library (c). **23 Alamy Images:** Mark Bourdillon (br); GL
Archive (tl); Peter Stroh (cr). **Corbis:** Bettmann (tr). **Fotolia:**
SM Web (c). **24 Corbis:** Bettmann (cr). **Dorling
Kindersley:** RAF Boulmer, Northumberland (bc). **Getty
Images:** Universal Images Group (cb). **24-25 Getty
Images:** The Washington Post (c). **25 Fotolia:** arquiplay77
(tr); Stephen Sweet (br). **26 Alamy Images:** Hilary Morgan
(cr). **Corbis:** Alinari Archives (cla). **TopFoto.co.uk:** Roger-
Viollet (br). **26-27 Alamy Images:** David Osborn (tc). **27
Dorling Kindersley:** Search and Rescue Hovercraft,
Richmond, British Columbia (bc). **Fotolia:** ijdema (br).
Getty Images: Frank Scherschel / Time & Life Pictures
(cb). **28 Corbis:** Bettmann (cl, bc). **Dorling Kindersley:**
The Science Museum, London (br). **28-29 NASA:** MIX (c).
29 Getty Images: Sovfoto / Universal Images Group (tc).
NASA: (cr, br). **30-31 NASA:** MIX (c). **30 Corbis:** Stocktrek
(bl). **31 Dorling Kindersley:** The Fleet Air Arm Museum
(bl). **Fotolia:** valdis torms (tr). **Pearson Asset Library:**
Oxford Designers & Illustrators Ltd. (cr). **Science Photo
Library:** Science Source (cla). **34 Alamy Images:** Interfoto
(cr, c); North Wind Picture Archives (bl). **Corbis:** Gianni
Dagli Orti (cl). **Fotolia:** Jonas Wolff (bc). **35 akg-images:**
(tl). **Alamy Images:** Interfoto (cl, c); (cl); (cb).
36-37 Dorling Kindersley: Saint Bride Printing Library,
London (c). **37 Corbis:** Stefano Bianchetti (c). **Dorling
Kindersley:** Penguin Books (bl). **Fotolia:** creative4m (br).
38 Alamy Images: Everett Collection Historical (c). **Corbis:**
Bettmann (crb). **Getty Images:** Apic / Hulton Archive (tr);
Science & Society Picture Library (cl/Sir Charles
Wheatstone). **Science & Society Picture Library:** Science
Museum (c). **39 Corbis:** Bettmann (tr). **Fotolia:** elypse (bl).
SuperStock: Eye Ubiquitous (cla). **40 Dorling Kindersley:**
The Science Museum, London (cl). **40-41 Corbis:**
Bettmann (c). **41 Corbis:** Bettmann (cl). **42 The
Bridgeman Art Library:** The Stapleton Collection (cb/Blue
legs). **Corbis:** Bettmann (bl). **Fotolia:** tony85 (cb/Gloves).
Getty Images: MPI / Archive Photos (cr); Science &
Society Picture Library (cb). **42-43 SuperStock:** Science
and Society. **43 The Bridgeman Art Library:** The Stapleton
Collection (clb/Pink legs). **Fotolia:** ojje11 (br); tony85 (cl/
Gloves, clb/Gloves); tony85 (clb/Gloves, clb/Gloves). **Mary
Evans Picture Library:** (clb). **44 Corbis:** Bettmann (bl).
Science Photo Library: Sheila Terry (cra); USA Library Of

Congress (br). **45-43 Getty Images:** Science & Society
Picture Library (c). **45 Getty Images:** Richards / Hulton
Archive (tr). **46 Corbis:** Michael Freeman (cl). **47 Getty
Images:** Digital Camera Magazine / Future (bc); George
Rose (tr). **48 Corbis:** Topic Photo Agency (cb). **Dorling
Kindersley:** Peter Wilson (bc). **Getty Images:** Science &
Society Picture Library (cl); William Vandivert / Time & Life
Pictures (c). **48-49 Dreamstime.com:** Les Palenik (tc).
NASA: (tc/Neil Armstrong). **49 Dreamstime.com:** Philcold
(br). **Fotolia:** imayda (clb); Maksym Yemelyanov (bc).
Photolibrary: image100 (clb/American football). **50
Corbis:** Bettmann (cla, cr). **Dorling Kindersley:** The
Science Museum, London (c, tr). **Dreamstime.com:** Patrick
Noonan (cl). **Getty Images:** Alfred Eisenstaedt / Time &
Life Pictures (c/William Shockley). **51 Dreamstime.com:**
Leonid Sadofiev (cb). **Getty Images:** Fotosearch / Archive
Photos (tl). **Photoshot:** UPPA (cl). **Science & Society
Picture Library:** Science Museum (c). **52 Dorling
Kindersley:** The Science Museum, London (cl). **Fotolia:**
Beboy (bc); Dmitry Vereshchagin (bl). **Getty Images:**
Science & Society Picture Library (c). **52-53 Fotolia:**
Gregor Buir (b). **Getty Images:** Hulton Archive (c). **53
Alamy Images:** Pictorial Press (tr); creative4m (tr)
(bl); mast3r (cr). **54 Dorling Kindersley:** The Science
Museum, London (bc, bl). **Getty Images:** Keystone-France
/ Gamma-Keystone (cl). **55 Corbis:** Bettmann (bl). **Fotolia:**
rekordkohle (cr). **56 Corbis:** Bettmann (cl). **Dorling
Kindersley:** The Science Museum, London (cb). **Fotolia:**
alexthewhale (br). **NASA:** GRIN (bl). **56-57 NASA and The
Hubble Heritage Team (AURA/STScl):** ESA / J. Hester and
A. Loll (Arizona State University) (c). **57 Dreamstime.com:**
Zrfphoto (br). **Getty Images:** Purestock (bl). **58 Corbis:**
Louie Psihoyos (cra). **Fotolia:** Cobalt (br, cr/Laptop);
indigolotos (cl/All images on the earth); senoldo (cra). **59
Corbis:** Andrew Brusso (tr). **Fotolia:** contrastwerkstatt (br).
62 Corbis: Bettmann (cb). **Getty Images:** Prisma /
Universal Images Group (cl). **62-63 Getty Images:** Science
& Society Picture Library (c). **63 Pearson Asset Library:**
HL Studios. (cra). **Photoshot:** LFI (bc). **64-65 Dreamstime.
com:** Almir1968 (tc). **64 Dreamstime.com:** Nicku (crb).
Getty Images: Peter Dazeley / Photographer's Choice (cl).
Pearson Asset Library: Coleman Yuen. **65 Alamy
Images:** Encyclopaedia Britannica / Universal Images
Group Limited (tr). **Dorling Kindersley:** National Maritime
Museum, London (clb). **66 Alamy Images:** Pictorial Press
Ltd (cla). **Corbis:** Hulton-Deutsch Collection (c). **Dorling
Kindersley:** The Science Museum, London (tr). **Fotolia:**
McCarthys_PhotoWorks (cl). **67 Corbis:** Bettmann (cra).
Fotolia: flariv (tl). **Getty Images:** Pierre Jahan / Roger
Viollet (cb). **Pearson Asset Library:** Gareth Boden (br); HL
Studios (cr). **68 Fotolia:** Denis Junker (br). **Getty Images:**
Science & Society Picture Library (clb, tr). **69 Corbis:**
Bettmann (cl). **Science & Society Picture Library:** Science
Museum (br). **70 Dreamstime.com:** Maxborovkov (tl).
Fotolia: Jeffrey Collingwood (cr); Ericos (bl); mitay20
(bc); photoguy_76 (cra). **Mary Evans Picture Library:** Karl
Sandels / IBL (cl). **70-71 Science & Society Picture
Library:** Science Museum (c). **71 Dreamstime.com:**
Maxborovkov (crb). **Fotolia:** fotoerre (bl); Piotr Pawinski
(bl). **Getty Images:** Universal Images Group (tl). **72 Corbis:**
Bettmann (tr); William G. Jackman (br). **Getty Images:**
AFP (bl); Science & Society Picture Library (cl). **73 Dorling
Kindersley:** The Science Museum, London (br). **Getty
Images:** Science & Society Picture Library (bl). **Pearson
Asset Library:** Oxford Designers & Illustrators Ltd (cra).
74-75 Dorling Kindersley: The Science Museum, London
(c). **74 Fotolia:** photosoft (br). **Science Photo Library:**
(clb). **75 Corbis:** Heritage Images (cb). **Dreamstime.com:**
Ademdemir (tl). **Fotolia:** ojje11 (br). **76 Dreamstime.com:**
Mohammed Anwarul Kabir Choudhury (c). **77
Dreamstime.com:** Fuzzbass (br); Shariff Che\' Lah (tr). **80
Alamy Images:** Zev Radovan / www.BibleLandPictures.
com (tr). **Fotolia:** Pixel Embargo (bl); koya979 (c). **81
Fotolia:** mrkob (br). **82 Getty Images:** Egyptian / The
Bridgeman Art Library (cla); Time & Life Pictures (bc).
Mary Evans Picture Library: (br). **82-83 Dreamstime.com:**
Romica (cl). **83 Alamy Images:** Chris Pancewicz (bl). **Mary
Evans Picture Library:** (tl). **84 Fotolia:** borilove (br). **85
Corbis:** Ted Spiegel (fbl). **Fotolia:** Lucky Dragon (c);
VERSUSstudio (fbl). **Science Photo Library:** (tl, cb). **86
Fotolia:** Zelfit (tl). **87 Dreamstime.com:** Vladyslav
Starozhylov (cl). **Fotolia:** christian42 (br). **88 Corbis:**
Stephan Goerlich / DPA (cr); Yumeto Yamazaki / AFLO /
Nippon News (bc). **Getty Images:** SSPL (c). **Science
Photo Library:** Peter Menzel (bl). **88-89 Science Photo
Library:** Peter Menzel (c). **89 Alamy Images:** Karen
Kasmauski / RGB Ventures LLC dba SuperStock (bc).
Corbis: © U.S. Navy - digital version copy / Science
Faction (tr). **Dorling Kindersley:** Department of

Cybernetics, University of Reading (bl). **90-91 Pearson
Asset Library:** Coleman Yuen. **91 Dreamstime.com:**
Martijn Mulder (br). **92 Fotolia:** haveseen (bl); Dario
Sabljak (tl). **The Granger Collection (tl/Levi
Strauss). 93 Corbis:** William G. Jackman (tc). **Fotolia:**
sergio37_120 (bl). **94 Dorling Kindersley:** The Royal
Academy of Music (b). **94-95 Dorling Kindersley:** The
National Music Museum (c). **95 Alamy Images:** Maurice
Savage (bl). **Corbis:** Sandro Vannini (c). **96 Alamy Images:**
Goimages (tr). **Dreamstime.com:** Pressureua (br). **Getty
Images:** Dennis Hallinan / Archive Photos (cl). **97 Corbis:**
Burger / Phanie / Phanie Sarl (bl). **Getty Images:**
Comstock Images (c). **98-99 Getty Images:** Science &
Society Picture Library (c). **98 Corbis:** Underwood &
Underwood (bl). **Dorling Kindersley:** Academy of Motion
Picture Arts and Sciences (br). **Getty Images:** Science &
Society Picture Library (cb). **99 Alamy Images:** Archives
du 7eme Art / Photos 12 (tl). **Dorling Kindersley:** Rough
Guides (tr). **Getty Images:** Silver Screen Collection /
Moviepix (bc). **100-101 Fotolia:** Sherri Camp (c). **100 The
Bridgeman Art Library:** Private Collection / Archives
Charmet (cl). **Corbis:** Ashley Cooper (br). **Dorling
Kindersley:** Armé Museum, Stockholm, Sweden (bl). **101
The Bridgeman Art Library:** The Stapleton Collection (tc).
Fotolia: Lucky Dragon (b). **Pearson Asset Library:** Debbie
Rowe (bc). **102 Getty Images:** Jay Paull / Archive Photos
(bl); Taylor S. Kennedy / National Geographic (cl).
SuperStock: Joachim E Röttgers / i / imagebroker.net (bc).
103 akg-images: Cameraphoto / Museo Civico Correr (tr).
Corbis: Olivier Polet (bc). **106 Corbis:** Bettmann (cl).
Dorling Kindersley: The Science Museum, London (t).
Getty Images: Medic Image / Universal Images Group (br).
107 Alamy Images: Pictorial Press Ltd (tl). **Getty Images:**
Jack Guez / AFP (crb). **Science & Society Picture Library:**
Science Museum (c). **108 Corbis:** Bettmann (bl). **Getty
Images:** UniversalImagesGroup (bc). **Science & Society
Picture Library:** Daily Herald Archive / National Media
Museum (cl). **Science Photo Library:** National Library Of
Medicine (c). **108-109 Dreamstime.com:** Strandtube (c).
109 Alamy Images: PF-(bygone1) (bl). **Corbis:** Bettmann
(tr). **Science Photo Library:** (cla). **110 Corbis:** Heritage
Images (bc); Tetra Images (tr). **Dorling Kindersley:** The
Science Museum, London (l). **Science Photo Library:** Eye
Of Science (cr). **111 Corbis:** Michael Rosenfeld / Science
Faction (tr). **Science Photo Library:** Matteis / Look At
Sciences (tl); Alexander Tsiaras (cb). **112 Fotolia:**
itsmejust (tl). **Getty Images:** Adam Gault / SPL (br). **113
Corbis:** (cr). **Fotolia:** Sven Bähren (tl). **Science Photo
Library:** Ria Novosti (tl). **114 Dreamstime.com:** Alptraum
(cb). **Getty Images:** Science & Society Picture Library
(cra). **115 Corbis:** Soren Svendsen / Nordicphotos (c).
Dorling Kindersley: The Science Museum, London (tl).
Dreamstime.com: Josetandem (clb). **116-117 Fotolia:** Eric
Isselee (c). **116 Dorling Kindersley:** The Science Museum,
London (bl). **Dreamstime.com:** Scott Griessel (c). **Getty
Images:** UniversalImagesGroup (bc). **Wellcome Images:**
Science Museum, London (bc). **117 Corbis:** Lebrecht /
Lebrecht Music & Arts (tr). **Dreamstime.com:** Pterwort
(cb). **Getty Images:** Bloomberg (bc). **Science Photo
Library:** Eye Of Science (bc); Sheila Terry (c). **118 The
Bridgeman Art Library:** Deutsches Historisches Museum,
Berlin, Germany / DHM (tr). **Getty Images:** Science &
Society Picture Library (cl). **119 Getty Images:** AFP (bl).
PunchStock: Brand X Pictures (cr). **Science Photo Library:**
Lawrence Lawry (tl). **120 Science Photo Library:** Physics
Today Collection / American Institute Of Physics (cl). **120-
121 Science Photo Library:** Manfred Kage (c). **121
Fotolia:** pzAxe (clb). **Science Photo Library:** Roger Harris
(cl); David Scharf (tr).

Jacket images: *Front:* **The Bridgeman Art Library:** The
Stapleton Collection bc/ (Pick legs), bc/ (Blue Legs);
Corbis: Hulton-Deutsch Collection cr/, Lawrence Manning
bc/ (Telephone), Lisa O'Connor / ZUMA Press tl; **Dorling
Kindersley:** National Maritime Museum, London cra,
National Maritime Museum, London ca; **Dreamstime.com:**
Cobalt88 tr; **Fotolia:** chones bl, Lucky Dragon cr, Gennady
Poddubny br, qingwa tc, tony85 bc/ (Gloves); **Getty
Images:** Hulton Archive cla, Science & Society Picture
Library cl, bc/ (Graham Bell); **Mary Evans Picture Library:**
bc; **Science Photo Library:** Sheila Terry tc/ (Guglielmo
Marconi); *Back:* **Corbis:** Brooks Kraft / Sygma clb, The
Mariners' Museum bl, Ocean cl; **Dorling Kindersley:**
National Cycle Collection fclb; **Dreamstime.com:** Kaarsten
clb/ (Body); **Fotolia:** Pixel Embargo tl, James Steidl cla;
Getty Images: MyLoupe / Universal Images Group cb;
NASA: MIX cr; **Science Photo Library:** Roger Harris tr,
Peter Menzel tc; *Spine:* **Dorling Kindersley:** The Science
Museum, London t.

All other images © Dorling Kindersley
For further information see: www.dkimages.com